HOWARD BRENTON

Howard Brenton was born in Portsmouth in 1942. His many
plays include *Christie in Love* (Portable Theatre, 1969);
Revenge (Theatre Upstairs, 1969); *Magnificence* (Royal Court
Theatre, 1973); *The Churchill Play* (Nottingham Playhouse,
1974, and twice revived by the RSC, 1978 and 1988); *Bloody
Poetry* (Foco Novo, 1984, and Royal Court Theatre, 1987);
Weapons of Happiness (National Theatre, Evening Standard
Award, 1976); *Epsom Downs* (Joint Stock Theatre, 1977); *Sore
Throats* (RSC, 1978); *The Romans in Britain* (National Theatre,
1980, revived at the Crucible Theatre, Sheffield, 2006);
Thirteenth Night (RSC, 1981); *The Genius* (1983), *Greenland*
(1988) and *Berlin Bertie* (1992), all presented by the Royal
Court; *Kit's Play* (RADA Jerwood Theatre, 2000); *Paul*
(National Theatre, 2005); *In Extremis* (Shakespeare's Globe,
2006 and 2007); *Never So Good* (National Theatre, 2008) and
The Ragged Trousered Philanthropists adapted from the novel
by Robert Tressell (Liverpool Everyman and Chichester
Festival Theatre, 2010).

Collaborations with other writers include *Brassneck* (with David
Hare, Nottingham Playhouse, 1972); *Pravda* (with David Hare,
National Theatre, Evening Standard Award, 1985) and *Moscow
Gold* (with Tariq Ali, RSC, 1990).

Versions of classics include *The Life of Galileo* (1980) and
Danton's Death (1982) both for the National Theatre, Goethe's
Faust (1995/6) for the RSC and a new version of *Danton's
Death* for the National Theatre (2010).

He wrote thirteen episodes of the BBC1 drama series *Spooks*
(2001–2005, BAFTA Best Drama Series, 2003).

Other Titles in this Series

Andrew Bovell
SPEAKING IN TONGUES
WHEN THE RAIN STOPS FALLING

Howard Brenton
BERLIN BERTIE
FAUST – PARTS ONE & TWO
    after Goethe
IN EXTREMIS
NEVER SO GOOD
PAUL
THE RAGGED TROUSERED
    PHILANTHROPISTS *after* Tressell

Jez Butterworth
JERUSALEM
MOJO
THE NIGHT HERON
PARLOUR SONG
THE WINTERLING

Caryl Churchill
BLUE HEART
CHURCHILL PLAYS: THREE
CHURCHILL: SHORTS
CLOUD NINE
A DREAM PLAY *after* Strindberg
DRUNK ENOUGH TO SAY
    I LOVE YOU?
FAR AWAY
HOTEL
ICECREAM
LIGHT SHINING IN
    BUCKINGHAMSHIRE
MAD FOREST
A NUMBER
SEVEN JEWISH CHILDREN
THE SKRIKER
THIS IS A CHAIR
THYESTES *after* Seneca
TRAPS

David Edgar
ALBERT SPEER
ARTHUR & GEORGE *after* Barnes
CONTINENTAL DIVIDE
EDGAR: SHORTS
THE MASTER BUILDER *after* Ibsen
PENTECOST
THE PRISONER'S DILEMMA
THE SHAPE OF THE TABLE
TESTING THE ECHO
A TIME TO KEEP *with* Stephanie Dale

Debbie Tucker Green
BORN BAD
DIRTY BUTTERFLY
RANDOM
STONING MARY
TRADE & GENERATIONS

Ayub Khan-Din
EAST IS EAST
LAST DANCE AT DUM DUM
NOTES ON FALLING LEAVES
RAFTA, RAFTA...

Liz Lochhead
BLOOD AND ICE
DRACULA *after* Bram Stoker
EDUCATING AGNES ('The School
    for Wives') *after* Molière
GOOD THINGS
MARY QUEEN OF SCOTS GOT
    HER HEAD CHOPPED OFF
MEDEA *after* Euripides
MISERYGUTS & TARTUFFE
    after Molière
PERFECT DAYS
THEBANS

Conor McPherson
DUBLIN CAROL
McPHERSON PLAYS: ONE
McPHERSON PLAYS: TWO
PORT AUTHORITY
THE SEAFARER
SHINING CITY
THE WEIR

Enda Walsh
BEDBOUND & MISTERMAN
DELIRIUM
DISCO PIGS & SUCKING DUBLIN
ENDA WALSH PLAYS: ONE
THE NEW ELECTRIC BALLROOM
PENELOPE
THE SMALL THINGS
THE WALWORTH FARCE

Nicholas Wright
CRESSIDA
HIS DARK MATERIALS *after* Pullman
MRS KLEIN
THE REPORTER
THÉRÈSE RAQUIN *after* Zola
VINCENT IN BRIXTON
WRIGHT: FIVE PLAYS

Howard Brenton

ANNE BOLEYN

NICK HERN BOOKS
London
www.nickhernbooks.co.uk

A Nick Hern Book

Anne Boleyn first published in Great Britain as a paperback original in 2010 by
Nick Hern Books Limited, 14 Larden Road, London W3 7ST

Reprinted in this revised edition in 2011

Anne Boleyn copyright © 2010 Howard Brenton

Howard Brenton has asserted his right to be identified as the author of this work

Cover image: Miranda Raison as Anne Boleyn, photograph by
Manuel Harlan, costume designed by Angela Davis
Cover design: Ned Hoste, 2H

Typeset by Nick Hern Books, London
Printed and bound in Great Britain by CLE Print Ltd, St Ives, Cambs,
PE27 3LE

A CIP catalogue record for this book is available from the British Library

ISBN 978 1 84842 099 1

Preface
Howard Brenton

Every year on the 19th of May flowers are delivered to the
Tower of London. Queen Anne Boleyn, Henry VIII's second
wife, was executed on that day in 1536. The flowers have been
arriving for forty years and no one knows who sends them.
They are put on the floor of the small Chapel of St Peter ad
Vincula, beneath which Anne's body – and head – were buried
in a wooden chest, without a plaque or stone. All traces of her
were then obliterated with a Stalinist ruthlessness: all of the
pictures, but perhaps for one, all of the images of her crest of
arms. Henry had his 'H' and her 'A' carved entwined on panels
and embossments throughout Hampton Court. They were all
removed – though one was missed: it can be seen in the Great
Hall, high up to the right on the wooden screen.

Today there is a fast-growing Anne Boleyn cult. She appeals
both to adolescents and to ageing romantics. Her story has a
Wagnerian intensity of love, death and betrayal, shot through
with a very un-Wagnerian sense of reckless fun, of daring
sexiness. But there is a deeper reason for the growing obsession
with her. The flowers acknowledge an unease; we love her story
but feel guilty toward her. I think I've understood why and it's
made me a paid-up cult member.

Anne was convicted of adultery, incest and treason. At her
trial she had been accused of being her brother's mistress, of
being a witch, of sleeping with a hundred men while married to
the King. She had been Queen for three years. In the glow of
her husband's devotion she was the most powerful woman in
the Kingdom, a force in her own right against whom no one
dared speak openly. But when the protective veil of the King's
affections evaporated she became 'the Concubine', the great
whore of the age. It was the Devil's work that she could not
give the King a male heir. Wild rumours spoke of her third

miscarriage delivering a fetus so distorted that the father must have been a succubus, a demon, even Old Nick himself. In the last days in the Tower, Anne went to pieces. But her wild spirit did not wholly desert her. From within her spinning hysteria she joked 'I shall have a nickname: Queen Anne the Headless'.

There are many Anne Boleyns. Popular culture – as in the television series *The Tudors* – sees her as a bright, sexy girl, manoeuvred by an ambitious father and his friends into the King's bed. Historians disagree. David Starkey sees her as 'a brutal and effective politician' who was, after all, able to bring down the King's First Minister, Cardinal Wolsey – whom she hated, ironically, for blocking a possible betrothal when she was younger. Antonia Fraser, who is very much of the Catholic party of Henry's first wife, the much put-upon and infuriatingly correct Catherine of Aragon, sees Anne as a schemer and a poseur. She accuses her of 'religious chic', always making sure she had a religious book in her hands when someone important came into the room. In her recent novel, *Wolf Hall*, Hilary Mantel gives us an extraordinary Anne, calculating yet instinctive, almost feral, a very dangerous woman indeed.

There is some truth, no doubt, in all these perceptions of her. Clearly she was formidable. When she was thirteen she was sent abroad, first to Burgundy then to Paris as a lady-in-waiting to the French Queen. Both Courts were notorious for political infighting; Anne observed and learnt. Her French became flawless; later, as favourite, then Queen, she made herself invaluable to Henry in the endless, convoluted negotiations with the French King.

By all accounts she was not a conventional beauty, but she seriously unnerved men. Perhaps it was a directness of gaze, a centred confidence, a charm without deference that bowled them over. She was also armed with a flashing and at times indiscreet wit and, when needed, a hell of a temper – she was, after all, the future mother of Elizabeth I.

When King Henry fell in love with her in 1526, she refused to sleep with him. She kept him hooked but at bay for nearly seven years while negotiations with the Pope to secure an annulment of Henry's marriage to Catherine foundered and then failed. The prurient Court gossips speculated, month by month, how far up Anne's thigh Henry was allowed to go. They finally slept together in Calais, a few weeks before they were married in great secrecy on the 25th of January 1533. Anne quickly became pregnant.

The cruelty of the past can be thrown into sharp relief by present-day knowledge. Anne gave birth to a healthy child, Elizabeth, and then had three miscarriages. Another historian, Alison Weir, argues that she was one of those rare women who are rhesus negative: when a man is rhesus positive and his partner negative, problems do not occur with the first child but they do with subsequent pregnancies. If Anne had given Henry and England a male heir, she would have been invulnerable. But she did not. Over Easter in 1536, Thomas Cromwell, the King's Chief Minister and at one time Anne's ally, decided to destroy her. It took him three weeks to launch a coup against her family and her faction, fix witnesses, rig a trial and have her dead.

So, an attractive and ambitious woman gets to the centre of a dangerous maze of male power to find there is only one way out: her death. It is a tragic and highly dramatic scenario and, as far as it goes, true. But it is a modern reading. There was a whole other dimension to Anne.

She was religious. More: she was a Protestant, a reformer, and an admirer of William Tyndale.

Tyndale's name provoked fear and loathing amongst both Catholics and moderate Protestants. He was in hiding on the outskirts of Antwerp (he was betrayed and publicly strangled and burnt in the same year as Anne's execution). His vivid, egalitarian translation of the Bible was banned, but copies were smuggled into England. Anne had one. She may well have been directly in touch with Tyndale. She certainly got hold of his *The Obedience of a Christian Man* when it was published in 1528. This was an explosive book, a key text of the Reformation, attacking the Pope and the Church. An incensed Cardinal Wolsey confiscated it from one of Anne's ladies-in-waiting. Anne went to the King and Wolsey was forced to return it. Anne marked up passages for Henry to read. He commented: 'This book is for me and for all kings to read.'

It is as if there was a Joan of Arc, driven by a religious vision, within the more familiar figure of Anne the dazzling sexual predator. She even died for religious reasons: she discovered Cromwell was stealing huge sums from the dissolution of the monasteries, money meant for the establishment of universities and religious schools. He moved so quickly because he feared she would tell the King.

Anne was in love with Henry but also in love with the most dangerous ideas of her day. She conspired to make England Protestant for ever. I am fascinated by heroes and heroines who were ahead of their time, like Abelard and Heloise in my first play for the Globe, *In Extremis*. Anne was one of them. She could not know the future, of course. But she helped detonate a religious upheaval which culminated a century later in the Civil War, the breaking of divine royal power and the establishment of our Parliament.

I wrote the play to celebrate her life and her legacy as a great English woman who helped change the course of our history.

This article was first published in the Independent *on 23 June 2010.*

Anne Boleyn was first performed at Shakespeare's Globe, London, on 24 July 2010, with the following cast:

ROBERT CECIL	Michael Bertenshaw
DEAN LANCELOT ANDREWES	Sam Cox
LADY JANE / SECOND COUNTRY WOMAN	Naomi Cranston
SIMPKIN / PARROT	John Cummins
GEORGE VILLIERS / FIRST COUNTRY MAN	Ben Deery
LADY CELIA / FIRST COUNTRY WOMAN	Mary Doherty
THOMAS CROMWELL	John Dougall
SLOOP / SINGER	Will Featherstone
KING JAMES I	James Garnon
WILLIAM TYNDALE	Peter Hamilton-Dyer
KING HENRY VIII	Anthony Howell
CARDINAL WOLSEY / HENRY BARROW	Colin Hurley
LADY ROCHFORD	Amanda Lawrence
ANNE BOLEYN	Miranda Raison
DOCTOR JOHN REYNOLDS	Dickon Tyrrell
SUPERNUMERARIES	Claire Bond, Nicole Hartley, Holly Morgan, Michael Curran, Michael Jarvis

Director   John Dove
Designer   Michael Taylor
Composer   William Lyons

The production was revived at the Globe in July 2011, with the following changes to the cast:

THOMAS CROMWELL	Julius D'Silva
LADY ROCHFORD	Sophie Duval
SUPERNUMERARIES	Claire Bond, Laura Darrall, Nicholas Delvale, Luke McConnell

Characters

ANNE BOLEYN
KING HENRY VIII
THOMAS CROMWELL
CARDINAL WOLSEY

LADY ROCHFORD ⎫
LADY CELIA ⎬ *Anne's women*
LADY JANE ⎭

SIMPKIN, *Cromwell's man*
SLOOP, *Wolsey's man; then Cromwell's*

WILLIAM TYNDALE

KING JAMES I
ROBERT CECIL
GEORGE VILLIERS
PARROT, *Cecil's man*

DEAN LANCELOT ANDREWES
DOCTOR JOHN REYNOLDS
HENRY BARROW

Plus
COUNTRY WOMEN ⎫
COUNTRY MEN ⎬ *followers of Tyndale*

DIVINES, COURTIERS, SERVANTS

*The action of the play takes place at the Court of King Henry
VIII (1527–1536) and the Court of King James I (1603–1604).*

*This text went to press before the end of rehearsals and so may
differ slightly from the play as performed.*

ACT ONE

Scene One

Enter ANNE BOLEYN *in her bloodstained execution dress. She has a large embroidered bag with her.*

ANNE (*aside. Working the audience*). Do you want to see it? Who wants to see it? Do you? You? I'll show then. (*Opens the bag.*) No, I won't. (*Closes the bag.*) I won't! I cannot see the advantage in it, and that was what I was taught, by Margaret of Burgundy, when I was thirteen, 'Know the advantage of everything, Anne.' And you won't like me for showing you, you'll say it's boastful, they said I was boastful, overweening. And why should I want you to love me? Did anyone around me ever love me, but for the King? So you can't see! You can't! (*Stamps her foot. Then laughs.*) Or would it be fun? Would it be a scandal? Better: would it make you laugh? Oh, that's all right then... here... (*Puts her hand in the bag.*) Ready? Look! (*Takes a Bible out of the bag.*) It's my Bible! Why? Don't you realise? This killed me! This book! This put me in the Tower, this made the sword, the sword, the sword... they played a trick. As I was kneeling. They made me look one way. And from the other way the sword... sang. In the air. For a second. I heard it sing, and... (*Pauses, then kisses the Bible and puts it back into the bag.*) What you think I was going to show you? This? (*Takes out her severed head.*) This? This? Funny, a head's smaller than you think. Heavy little cabbage, that's all. Let me show you something. Eyes closed, see? (*Pulls the eyelids up with her fingers.*) For a moment I saw my body lying in the straw. And I closed my eyes. It was I, closing them.

She closes the eyes on the head. She stands, the head under her arm.

And now I'm with Jesus. I am! I'll bring you all to Jesus.

Enter KING JAMES I *followed by* LORD ROBERT CECIL.

ANNE *points at* JAMES.

He won't. James the Sixth of Scotland, sixty-seven years after my – (*Gestures.*) come to rule you all. James the Sixth of Scotland. Now James the First of England. But he won't bring you to Jesus.

She skips away and exits.

Scene Two

JAMES *and* CECIL. CECIL*'s man* PARROT *lurks.*

Listening COURTIERS *edge as close as they dare to try to overhear.*

JAMES. Two thousand dresses!

CECIL. Yes, Your Majesty.

JAMES. Elizabeth had two thousand dresses?

CECIL. Her late Majesty knew the importance of the pomp of princes.

JAMES. The pimp of princes.

CECIL. Pomp, Your Majesty.

JAMES. The pomping and pimping of princes. (*Laughs.*) Two thousand dresses. We have come out of Scotland to a world of marvels.

CECIL. You come, Sire, a King of Scotland and rightful heir to the English throne. For the Kingdom was cast into darkness, the sun of Eliza set, her people were cast into darkness and cold. But now from the north a new sun has arisen, Your Majesty from Scotland ascends the throne, light floods the rejoicing towns and villages, warmth returns, a new glory and light shines upon us.

JAMES (*makes a farting noise*). Oh, I do believe I ripped a fart.

CECIL. Your Majesty?

JAMES. No, not a fart, it was a flash of light from my arse illuminating England.

CECIL. Your Majesty, I...

JAMES. No no no, tum tum tum, you spoke smoothly, My Lord Cecil. Smoothly, smotherly.

CECIL. I assure Your Majesty that...

JAMES. You see, I come from a more primitive world. I was brought up amongst the terrorism of great lords. In Edinburgh I looked for courtiers with knives in their sleeves. Here, I think, the danger is from words in their mouths.

CECIL. But I must protest my sincerity...

JAMES. Yum tum! Where are they?

CECIL. Your Majesty?

JAMES. The dresses! That woman's dresses!

CECIL. I have picked the best. (*Claps his hands.*) Come!

    CECIL *peels away.*

PARROT (*low, to* CECIL). The dresses, My Lord? I was going to sell them.

CECIL. Don't tell me.

PARROT. The servants in the hall expect something on the side.

CECIL. Enough.

PARROT. It's a once-in-a-generation opportunity, My Lord. A change of monarch. Get your hands on a few souvenirs.

CECIL. I let you have the pewter plate.

PARROT. None of the silver, though.

CECIL. What?

PARROT. Nothing, My Lord.

Enter SERVANTS, *their arms full of dazzling dresses. They pile them in front of* JAMES. CECIL *fusses about, displaying them. One* SERVANT *also pulls a chest onto the stage.*

JAMES *speaks aside as this happens.*

JAMES (*aside*). For three years this Englishman wrote to me in secret, with Elizabeth slowly dying. Who would I keep in my Privy Chamber? Why, all of you, My Lords, no need for jostling, assassination. I've seen enough jostles and killings. Did the old woman name me her successor to the throne? Cecil says yes. But I doubt that. And for a month I came down from Edinburgh, staying in the great English houses, hunting, feasting. I hanged a man in Newark, perhaps a mistake. But let the Sassenach see a gesture, a move of the new royal hand. And when I came to London: thousands in the streets, cries of joy and welcome. And here I stand, suddenly... rich.

JAMES *pauses, still, staring at nothing.* CECIL *coughs.* JAMES *comes back to life. He fingers a dress.*

Government by a show of glory. Elizabeth understood that very well. But glory is not enough, is it, to govern. There must also be... one mind. And fear. Tum tum.

CECIL. Er... There is another garment. We found it in Her late Majesty's private closet, locked away.

A SERVANT *opens the chest.* JAMES *looks into it. He lifts a superb, jewel-encrusted dress.*

JAMES. An old style.

He holds the dress against himself. He sweeps a half turn.

Now this is glory. Made, no doubt, for some great occasion?

CECIL (*embarrassed by* JAMES *holding the dress*). Yes. A coronation.

JAMES. This is Elizabeth's coronation dress? (*Caresses it.*)

CECIL. No. Her mother's.

JAMES (*holding the dress against him*). Anne Boleyn, the harlot Queen herself, crowned in this?

CECIL. There was a miniature with it...

He holds out a miniature on a chain. JAMES *steadies it for a moment, peering.*

JAMES. Ah. The Boleyn swan neck, still in the night thoughts of young men. The pure white curve of skin, across it the line of the blade blossoming with blood.

JAMES stares on. CECIL *coughs.* JAMES *comes out of it.*

She was crowned in this? That witch's body, folded within these very creases? (*Laughs.*) Think... (*Lifting the hem up his leg.*) The hem slid up to the thigh by the hand of the great Henry himself. There could even be... (*Lifts the dress right up, looking on the underside.*) interesting stains.

JAMES ruffles through the underside of the skirt, intent on what he is doing.

CECIL. Your Majesty, er...

He is ignored. JAMES *suddenly buries his face in the dress and sniffs, deeply.*

(*Aside.*) I put this man on the throne of England. What have I done?

JAMES. Vile! Vile! The stink of witchcraft! (*Throws the dress down on the chest.*) Burn it.

CECIL. At once, Your Majesty.

JAMES. No, leave it! (*Peering into the chest.*) What else is in there? The Boleyn woman's head? (*Laughs.*)

CECIL. Nothing else was found...

But the hyperactive JAMES *is all over the chest, kicking it, thumping it, kneeling beside it, hitting the inside with a dagger.*

JAMES. All our secrets in hiding places, through the dangerous years. The lies we think are truths, behind tapestries, loose stones in stairwells, false drawers...

CECIL. Your Majesty, perhaps help...

JAMES *rips out the bottom of the chest and throws it away. He stands, two small books, bound in black leather, in his hands. He opens one.*

JAMES. A New Testament? (*Turns to the title page.*) This is William Tyndale's translation! And she has written her name within: 'Anne B. by the mercy of Christ...'

CECIL. Tyndale? He was a fanatic.

JAMES. But a great scholar. (*Flicking through the small book, intent on it.*) He translated from the original Greek. Erasmus's fine edition, I have it...

CECIL. Scholar or not, the man was a dangerous agitator, Sire. They did burn him, when they caught him...

JAMES. Oh, no doubt he was a highly agitational, burnable pain in the bum. See, he had the Testament printed octavo size, small in the hand. To be smuggled into the country. (*To the title page again.*) 'Anne B. by the mercy of Christ...' Woman, what were you doing with this? (*Raises the book to his face and sniffs it.*)

CECIL. Many do hold it to be an heretical translation, Your Majesty.

JAMES. Oh, it is. He translates 'king' as 'tyrant' a little too often. (*Holds it up by a corner, the pages open.*) Grey paper between slabs of rough leather. But out of it, peace, the Word of God? No no no. Because of little books like this: minds turned molten with heresy, rebellion, cities on fire, the death of kings. What is the most dangerous threat to a kingdom? War, plague, poverty, ambitious men? No no no. Nothing can tear a country apart like religion. I know. I was brought up amongst Presbyterians.

He laughs. Then bad-temperedly throws the book back into the chest.

Tum tum tum tum. We must settle religion in England.

CECIL (*aside*). Perhaps not a fool. Or: the wisest fool in Christendom.

JAMES *opens the second book. He is dead still.*

JAMES. Bring me some wine.

CECIL. Sire, may I ask what...

JAMES. No. This is reading for a king. Go.

He wanders away, intent on the unidentified book. CECIL *gestures to the* SERVANTS, *who clear the dresses and the chest.*

CECIL (*to* PARROT). Master Parrot!

PARROT. My Lord.

CECIL. There was a book in the chest.

PARROT. We went over the chest very thoroughly, there was only the dress and a locket...

CECIL. There was a hidden compartment.

PARROT. We didn't find it.

CECIL. Obviously not! But His Majesty did! I showed him the chest as a novelty, something to amuse, to... prevent Scottish gloom descending. And what does he do? Tear it apart and find a Bible and a book!

PARROT. My Lord...

CECIL. A book he is now reading! It's dangerous when monarchs read books. They should stick with hunting and horses.

PARROT. My Lord, if I'd have found the book I'd have stolen it, wouldn't I, and there'd be no problem...

CECIL. Oh, go go! Give someone a whipping for not searching the chest. And thank your star it's not you.

PARROT (*aside*). That's how it works. Punishment flows downward, from the Lord to the likes of me to the likes of you. But we all know our place. The mighty and the mice...

PARROT *quickly exits.*

JAMES *is reading, a glass of wine in his hand.*

JAMES (*without looking up*). George! George! Come, boy, come, come! Slip out of the shadows or wherever you're lurking.

GEORGE VILLIERS *comes from behind a pillar. A very fit young man, fashionably dressed.*

GEORGE. Very graciously Your Majesty told me to be in attendance.

JAMES. And attending you were, boy. No doubt to every word?

GEORGE. Your Majesty, I would never...

JAMES. Never never, no? Oh, no, tum tum. If you won't listen you will never be of any use, and use you should be put to, George.

GEORGE. I am, from my heart, most grateful to Your Majesty. To wait upon the newly risen sun is...

JAMES (*interrupts*). Wait with nothing up your sleeve?

GEORGE. Your Majesty?

JAMES. No, if you have a knife, it'll be in your mouth. Will you cut me with your mouth, George?

GEORGE. I...

JAMES. What do you like to read?

GEORGE (*a panicky look*). I enjoy *The Romance of the Rose*.

JAMES. Steamy stuff. Ladies in towers, knights with their manhood bulging against their armour? Shall I call you Steamy?

Two listening COURTIERS *giggle.*

GEORGE. Your Majesty can call anyone anything.

JAMES. Yes, yes, I can, can't I! Ha! Tum tum!

CECIL (*aside*). God preserve us!

They look at each other.

JAMES. Steamy, Steamy, tell me, you're from common English stock, no?

GEORGE. My father was a gentleman, Sire. And my mother sent me to France for an education.

JAMES. Where you learnt the reading of romances, in French.

GEORGE. Well, not really in French... more in English... translation.

JAMES. Ah. So what were the benefits of your sojourn amongst that snooty, 'look down upon us all as barbarians' race?

GEORGE. Well... The fencing was very good and the dancing. And it's very useful being able to eat a whole chicken. With all the bones.

JAMES. You learnt that from the French?

GEORGE. No, from being brought up in Leicestershire. But it mightily impressed the frogs.

JAMES. You seek to impress, do you, Steamy?

GEORGE. I...

JAMES. No matter, you do. I suspect more than you realise. Oh, Steamy, how much do you know yourself? Because, looking at you, I wonder... exactly how devious *are* the English? Do I have to learn a whole new lexicon of deceit, south of the border?

GEORGE. I...

JAMES. Put it another way. Do you have any depth in you at all?

GEORGE. We try not to do depth in Leicestershire.

JAMES. I am greatly relieved to hear it.

GEORGE (*aside*). So this is how it is with him. I'll tell people he calls me 'steany' with an 'n'. That they are mishearing it with an 'm'.

JAMES. Steamy, as an English reader of love stories, what do you make of this? (*Hands the book to* GEORGE.)

GEORGE (*reads the title page*). *The Obedience of a Christian Man*.

JAMES. It's a book by William Tyndale.

GEORGE (*hot coals*). Is it banned?

JAMES. Oh, yes. Written eighty years ago and still fit for the fire. Read a page. It's very romantic.

GEORGE. Romantic? A book by William Tyndale?

JAMES. Look. (*Takes the book and opens a page, gives it back*.)

GEORGE. There's handwriting, down the edge...

JAMES. Yes, yes! Read it!

GEORGE. 'My loving Lord, as much as you desire that I will...'

JAMES. It's Boleyn! Anne Boleyn! Writing to King Henry!

GEORGE. The Concubine...

JAMES. Oh, yes!

GEORGE. Is it witchcraft?

JAMES. Good question, Leicestershire. She gave him this book. Why? To warp him? To make his mind moil and dither? Let's ask her.

GEORGE. But she's... (*A gesture, edge of hand to neck*.)

JAMES. A spirit done great violence to can live on. She's with us here, now.

GEORGE (*looks about*). What? Without her...?

JAMES. She dances, she laughs. In this old Palace. It belonged to a great man she ruined, and Henry gave it to her, all this magnificence. (*Arms around* GEORGE.) Sh! Listen!

ANNE *laughs, offstage*.

GEORGE. Oh, angels save us...

JAMES. Angels? Are you Catholic, Steamy?

GEORGE. No no, Sire. Not theological at all. Church of England.

JAMES. Good man. Oh, for a country full of you, everyone in church on their knees without really knowing why. Ha! (*Change*.) But Boleyn the witch will not have it so. She will not have the country rest. Come come come, let's find her!

Again ANNE *laughs, offstage.*

JAMES *pulls* GEORGE *away.*

Witches can fly. Do you think she can fly? Anne, you hussy! Where are you? Anne!

GEORGE (*aside*). A ghost hunt?

They exit.

Scene Three

Enter ANNE, LADY ROCHFORD *and four* LADIES *in high spirits. They are masked. They throw oranges to and at each other, catching some, missing others. They call out the names of parts they are to play in a masque.*

ANNE. Beauty!

CELIA. Me!

ROCHFORD. Me me! Constancy!

JANE. Me me! Kindness!

ROCHFORD (*pointing*). Mercy!

CELIA (*pointing*). Honour!

JANE. Pity!

ANNE (*throwing oranges to other* LADIES). Loyalty! Pity!

Laughter, screams. Oranges flying about the stage.

Before they realise it, KING HENRY VIII *enters, catching an orange.*

HENRY. Learning your parts for the masque, my ladies?

They all bow very low, faces looking down. And stay down.

And what virtue of womanhood are you to play, Mistress Anne?

She hesitates.

Don't think you can disguise yourself. I know that Boleyn flash of ankle.

LADY ROCHFORD *sneaks a glance at* ANNE.

ANNE. Your Majesty.

HENRY. So what is your part?

ANNE. I am Perseverance, Your Majesty.

HENRY. Is that a virtue?

ANNE. It is love's greatest, Your Majesty.

HENRY. I'd have thought kindness, or mercy to the pleas of a suitor, the greatest virtues in a woman's love. Or am I to be corrected?

ANNE. You are, Sire. Kindness can go lukewarm to cold, mercy can save only to dismiss. But perseverance gives love an undying flame.

A moment.

HENRY. My my. The stuff of courtly love! Your father sent you to France, didn't he?

ANNE. I had the honour to be placed in the service of Her Majesty the Queen of France.

HENRY. At what age?

ANNE *hesitates.*

Your history! Give me that, if nothing else.

ANNE. My father first sent me to the Court of Queen Margaret of Burgundy when I was thirteen. I went to France when I was fifteen. I was there for three years.

HENRY. Ah. Margaret of Burgundy then the Queen of France.
You've been schooled by powerful women.

ANNE. Your Majesty.

HENRY. I wonder what you learnt. (*Claps his hands.*) Come,
we'll begin! 'The Masque of the Green Chateau'! You ladies
play the womanly virtues, defending the battlements. We
men play the manly virtues, storming them! You will repulse
us as best you can, with these. (*Holds up an orange and
laughs.*) I will be Amorousness! Then we will all go to
dinner and afterwards: dance!

He exits. The WOMEN *stand. The others step back from*
ANNE, *afraid of her. The King's attentions have transformed
her status.*

Music strikes up.

ANNE. What?

ROCHFORD. Make sure you're at the top of the Chateau. If he
climbs up to you, then it's yours.

ANNE. What is?

ROCHFORD. Don't play the innocent.

ANNE. The King ruined my sister.

ROCHFORD. She's not ruined! She's living in luxury.

ANNE. But in the country. And married off to a man she hates
and she's still in love with the King.

ROCHFORD. You can't say no to him, Anne.

ANNE. Maybe not. But there are many ways of saying 'yes'.

She laughs and takes LADY ROCHFORD's *hand. The music
is louder. They exit, running.*

Scene Four

Music and laughter offstage.

Enter THOMAS CROMWELL *and* CARDINAL WOLSEY.
Their men, SIMPKIN *and* SLOOP, *hover at a distance.*

WOLSEY. Who was the one the King clambered up to?

CROMWELL. The Lady Anne Boleyn.

WOLSEY (*grunts*). I was terrified he was going to fall.

CROMWELL. Steps were discreetly put into the wall of the
wooden tower so His Majesty could make his assault.

WOLSEY. How much did all this cost?

CROMWELL. Twenty pounds.

WOLSEY. Twenty pounds!? To have a bunch of women throw
fruit at you?

CROMWELL. Youth must have its hour, Your Grace.

WOLSEY. The trouble is, His Majesty's hour of youth is
stretching into years. Ah well. (*Turns to go. Stops.*) Did you
say *Anne* Boleyn?

CROMWELL. Anne, yes.

WOLSEY. The sister of the one he had last year?

CROMWELL. Yes.

WOLSEY. Had the mother too, didn't he?

CROMWELL. Only for a night.

WOLSEY. God's teeth! Is he working his way through the
whole family? You're sure it was the Boleyn girl? Young
women all seem the same to me, masks on or off.

CROMWELL. I glimpsed the ankle.

WOLSEY. You think it will last?

CROMWELL. No.

WOLSEY. Soiled goods?

CROMWELL. She was educated in France.

WOLSEY (*grunts*). What about the father, watching the Royal Prerogative work its way up his family's skirts?

CROMWELL. Sir Thomas is… flexible.

WOLSEY. All the same, better look out an honour or two, to keep him flexed. In a bent-over position.

They laugh.

What concerns me. (*Beat.*) What concerns me is the loveliest of all who is not here tonight.

CROMWELL. Yes.

WOLSEY. Is the Queen even in the Palace?

CROMWELL. She went by barge to Richmond this morning.

WOLSEY. You can't blame her. To sit watching her husband climb wooden towers after twenty-year-olds? You have someone close to her?

CROMWELL. Oh, yes, one of her ladies reports to me every night.

WOLSEY (*grunts*). Are your eyes and ears everywhere, Master Cromwell?

CROMWELL (*bows*). I am pleased to be of service.

Offstage, ANNE *laughs.*

WOLSEY. We'll go back to York House and do some work. I can't stand the stench of lust in these rooms, even the tapestries reek of it.

They exit.

Scene Five

HENRY *and* ANNE *enter.* LADY ROCHFORD *and* ANNE'*s* COURT LADIES *observe from one place,* SIMPKIN *and* SLOOP *from another.*

ANNE *still has the mask. She and* HENRY *stand looking at each other for a moment.*

HENRY. You hit me on the nose with an orange.

ANNE. Your Majesty was storming the castle.

HENRY. Not the castle, storming you.

ANNE. All the more reason for you to be hit on the nose. Sire.

HENRY. You were too warlike! It was a pastime, all in good company.

ANNE. 'Company can be good or ill...'

ANNE / HENRY. '...But every man has his free will.'

HENRY. You're quoting one of my songs!

ANNE. Then be instructed by it, Sire.

HENRY. How?

ANNE. Give up rough pastimes.

HENRY. But that's what life is, Lady Anne! A rough pastime: hunt, sing, dance, make war, make love. That's where my heart is set.

ANNE. On roughness?

HENRY. I must have some dalliance.

ANNE. Dalliance is idleness.

HENRY. Dalliance is youth. Which I still have in me. Do I not? Answer carefully.

ANNE. You do still have great youth in you, Sire. Sadly.

HENRY. Sadly?

ANNE. Youthful dalliance is the chief mistress of vices.

HENRY. I'm only flirting with you, Anne! Don't lecture me.

ANNE. I'm not lecturing you, Sire. I'm displaying disdain. In courtly love, isn't that what the woman does? (*Curtsies low, bowing her head.*) Display disdain?

HENRY. My, my. What do we have here?

He holds his hand out. She takes it and rises, still looking down.

How can I win your love, Anne?

ANNE (*and she looks at him*). By perseverance.

HENRY. Then I will persevere. For as long as it takes. How long will that be? An hour?

ANNE. Oh, I think a little longer.

HENRY. Let me be plain as the simplest song, gentle as the night air through that window, clear as the moonlight in the orchards below; plain, gentle and clear as these words: honour me.

He pulls her to him.

ANNE. Forgive me, Your Majesty, but songs end, air can chill, moonlight casts dark shadows.

HENRY. Pretty, Anne, very pretty.

ANNE. As pretty as your words.

HENRY. Enough of courtly stuff! Mistress, come to bed.

He embraces her, roughly. She yields for a moment then pushes away.

ANNE. I beseech Your Highness, most earnestly, to desist.

HENRY. Desist? Why?

ANNE. Your Highness, please, take my answer in good part.

HENRY. Part? What part?

ANNE. I... I would rather lose my life than my honesty.

HENRY. This is highly original of you, Anne. (*A moment.*) I could force you, you know.

ANNE. Yes, Your Majesty.

HENRY. Overpower you.

ANNE. Yes, Your Majesty.

HENRY. But I can't, can I. Why not, why? Have you hexed me?

She keeps dead still, looking directly into his eyes.

You have. Overpower you and I lose my power. What are you?

ANNE. I am Perseverance, my love.

A pause, staring at each otl er. Then he lets her go and backs away.

HENRY. Oh dear, oh dear. (*Laughs.*) Oh dear, oh dear, oh dear. Am I lost?

Music. Dancing couples. ANNE *and* HENRY *join in.*

The dance disperses. Exit HENRY *and* DANCERS. ANNE *and* LADY ROCHFORD *stay on the stage.*

Scene Six

LADY ROCHFORD *and* ANNE. *Enter two* COURT LADIES *with a dress. During the scene,* ANNE *changes.*

ROCHFORD (*low*). Anne, the King's sent you a letter. (*Holds it out.*) Here...

ANNE. Wait.

ROCHFORD (*to the* COURT LADIES). Leave us.

The COURT LADIES *exit but sneak back to try to overhear.*

Dressing continues. Enter HENRY. *He has a quill pen and a half-written letter.*

HENRY (*aside*). Of all the hateful things in life, writing a letter is one of the worst. Rather have another wound in my leg than… Oh well. (*Reads his letter.*) 'Dearest Heart.' (*Looks up.*) No, weak, weak. I like to write lyrics to songs, they don't have to mean anything. But prose, you have to say what you mean. But I daren't write down what I really mean. Because she may reject me, which is obviously unthinkable. And because… because what I want to say is: 'Anne, come to my private rooms, stand in the candlelight, white in your nightdresses, then lift them high over your head, let them slip to the floor, then slip yourself into the soft linen of my bed, lay your slender shoulder against the goose-down pillows, and turn to me beneath the warm bear-fur cover, and let me hold the naked length of you against me.'

A moment. He looks at the letter again.

Rather ripe. But I'll write it, in as many words. Can't go round all day long with a hard-on. (*Laughs.*) 'Madam…'

He wanders away, studying his letter.

ANNE *is dressed. She snatches the letter and opens it. She reads.*

HENRY *reads as if checking the letter, pacing about.*

'Madam. If it shall please you to do me the office of a true, loyal mistress…'

ROCHFORD. Oh, Anne!

HENRY. '…and give yourself up, body and soul, to me who will be and have been your loyal servant…'

ANNE. '…I promise you that not only shall the name be given you…'

ANNE / HENRY. '…but that also I will take you for my only mistress, rejecting from thought and affection all others save yourself, to serve you only.'

HENRY (*aside*). That should do it.

Exit HENRY.

ROCHFORD. Anne, your life has changed.

ANNE. But has the world, Jane?

ROCHFORD. What do you mean?

ANNE. Pray with me.

ROCHFORD. I think you should go to your bath, not your prayers. Scent yourself with rose water, not church incense? (*Lower*.) And you need devices.

ANNE. Devices? (*Realises*.) Oh.

LADY ROCHFORD *gestures to the two* COURT LADIES, *who rush forward*.

ROCHFORD. You must know the French way. Vinegar in balls of wool.

ANNE. It stings the woman and the man horribly. They say.

ROCHFORD. There are English methods.

ANNE. I dread to imagine.

ROCHFORD (*to one of the* COURT LADIES). Celia. Give me your devices.

CELIA. Is it safe?

ROCHFORD. Yes.

The WOMEN *look around. Then* CELIA *takes out five little wooden blocks. She holds them out in the palm of her hand*.

ANNE. Little blocks of wood?

ROCHFORD. Yes.

ANNE. You put these…?

ROCHFORD. Yes.

ANNE. Ouch.

JANE. You mean you...

They look at her for a moment.

ROCHFORD. There are other ways. Celia?

CELIA *takes out two amulets and holds them out.* ANNE *takes them, cautiously.*

ANNE. What is this?

CELIA. The anus of a hare.

ANNE. And this?

CELIA. The testicles of a weasel.

ANNE. What do you do with...

CELIA. Why, wear them on your wrist, when... when you are with a man.

A pause.

ANNE. This is witchcraft.

ROCHFORD. Men call it that. But we have to survive at Court. With the men. You know this, Anne!

ANNE. I won't talk about this.

ROCHFORD (*pulling* ANNE *away*). You must. The King already has a bastard son. The Queen barely tolerates him. For a new mistress to have a child would be dangerous.

ANNE. Oh, I'll do dangerous.

ROCHFORD. What do you mean?

ANNE. I mean I'll have true love or nothing at all.

ROCHFORD. True love, what is that?

ANNE. Love with a Christian man.

ROCHFORD. I thought you were clever, Anne.

ANNE. True love with a true Christian man. Which he is.

ROCHFORD. Christian he may be, but a man he is not...

ANNE.... Oh, I don't think he lacks...

ROCHFORD. I mean he is more than a man, he is a king!

ANNE. I am not going to be a mistress! No fiddling with womanly devices. No bathing in scents and rose water.

ROCHFORD. Anne, you'd be ruined. You'd have to go into a convent...

ANNE. I will say 'yes' to the King's desires. But 'no' to his bed. I will say to my love: 'Yes, but when...'

ROCHFORD. When what?

ANNE *smiles*. LADY ROCHFORD *gets it*.

You can't. You can't seriously set out to do that. It won't work!

ANNE. Catherine's past child-bearing age.

ROCHFORD. No.

ANNE. She's not given him a son.

ROCHFORD. Marriages are made by God.

ANNE. That one wasn't. It was made by the Pope.

ROCHFORD. You can't think that!

ANNE. I can. I do. I will be a new Queen. For a new England.

ROCHFORD. I think you really had better go and pray.

ANNE. Jane. It could be God's Will.

ROCHFORD. Your will!

ANNE. God's Will. This may be his purpose for me on earth. (*Low*.) A Protestant Queen for England.

ROCHFORD. You terrify me, Anne. I love you and you terrify me.

Scene Seven

ANNE *and* LADY ROCHFORD *stay on stage. Enter* HENRY, WOLSEY, CROMWELL *and* SIMPKIN.

LADY ROCHFORD *and* SIMPKIN *hover.*

HENRY *seated. All the others stand.*

ANNE (*aside, front of the stage*). Five years later.

She turns and paces up and down.

HENRY. All right all right all right! In the name of all the Saints, why does the Queen need counsel?

WOLSEY. It is a divorce court, My Lord. If it were a criminal court, Her Majesty could of course be denied the right to speak. But technically she is not on trial...

HENRY. Oh, technically technically... when will I be rid of 'technically' and free to live?

CROMWELL (*low to* WOLSEY). Be careful, Your Grace, signs of an explosion...

WOLSEY. Your Majesty, it is irksome. But I know you only seek truth in the eyes of Almighty God in this matter.

HENRY. I do, Wolsey, I do.

WOLSEY. The Queen must make her arguments. The Court will recommend the annulment of your marriage...

HENRY. My illegal marriage...

WOLSEY. ... your illegal marriage...

HENRY. ... Marriage illegal in the sight of God, against nature and forbidden in Scripture. Leviticus 20, 21.

ANNE (*gritting her teeth*). Leviticus Leviticus, I am sick of Leviticus.

c. wife

HENRY. 'If a man shall take his brother's life, it is an unclean thing: he hath uncovered his brother's nakedness: they shall be childless.'

WOLSEY. An illegal marriage, incestuous, yes...

HENRY. I married my brother's wife! That is offensive in Heaven itself, Wolsey!

WOLSEY. Yes, Your Majesty. All I am trying to do is make it equally offensive on Earth.

HENRY. And taking until the last trump to do it!

WOLSEY. This will work, Your Majesty. Cardinal Campeggio will commend the Court's findings to His Holiness, the marriage will be annulled and Your Majesty will be free.

ANNE (*to* LADY ROCHFORD). It won't work!

She turns away.

HENRY. Lady Anne, stop walking up and down like that! It is more than I can bear!

ANNE. And being still is more than I can bear!

WOLSEY *and* CROMWELL *glance at each other.*

HENRY. Oh, apoplexy, apoplexy! It would be a relief!

ANNE. My Lord, forgive me.

She curtsies low, LADY ROCHFORD *with her.*

HENRY. Where were we? Oh, yes: the Queen's counsels. Who are they?

CROMWELL *hands* WOLSEY *a paper. A little confusion, they consult.*

ROCHFORD (*low to* ANNE). Be careful, say nothing.

ANNE. I'll never say anything against Catherine. Ever. I just wish the bitch would piss off to a convent.

ROCHFORD. Anne!

ANNE. All right all right all right!

HENRY (*to* WOLSEY). Well? Well?

WOLSEY. Her Majesty will be represented in the Legatine Court by William Wareham, Archbishop of Canterbury.

The names incense ANNE.

By Doctor Henry Standish, Bishop of London. By John Clerk, Bishop of Bath and Wells, and by John Fisher, Bishop of Durham.

ANNE. Fisher! That snake!

They stare at her.

HENRY (*standing*). Your Grace, we will continue with this later.

WOLSEY (*bows*). Your Majesty.

They all bow. HENRY *paces, watched by* ANNE. *She gestures to* LADY ROCHFORD, *who curtsies to* HENRY *and leaves.*

He's angry with her. Maybe...

CROMWELL. Don't get your hopes up. They're like an old married couple already.

HENRY *and* ANNE *on another part of the stage, pacing about.*

HENRY. Don't start, Anne!

ANNE. *I'm* not going to 'start'. It's always *you* who 'start'.

WOLSEY. Intolerable woman. (*Closer.*) Thomas, is it true that when she was at the French Court, she fell in with a nest of heretics? Protestants? That one was her lover and turned her toward Luther and his Antichrist doctrines?

CROMWELL. People say anything they like about her, Your Grace. She's a witch, she's a demon whose true form is a goat, appearing in a woman's form to ensnare the King...

WOLSEY (*grunts*). Hunh. Terrifying thing, the popular imagination. You know nothing about her and Protestants in France?

CROMWELL. Nothing, Your Grace.

WOLSEY. You're my intelligencer, Thomas. I rely on you.

CROMWELL (*bows*). Your Grace. (*Aside*.) I'm lying. I know everything about her in France.

WOLSEY *and* CROMWELL *exit*.

ANNE. Nothing will come of this ridiculous Court.

HENRY. You don't see the full matter. Leave it to your betters.

ANNE. You mean bishops?

HENRY. The Legatine Court is the best hope for an annulment. His Grace the Cardinal Campeggio will be here in a month.

ANNE. I met Cardinal Campeggio. Ten years ago, in France. He was already senile then. He dribbled.

HENRY. It doesn't really matter if he dribbles or not! All he has to do is take the Court's decision to the Pope. And the Court will decide for my divorce.

ANNE. Really? How?

HENRY. Anne, this matter is complex, it is theological, it is High Church politics and it is beyond a woman's brain!

ANNE. It's not beyond your wife's brain. She understands it all too well. She got her uncle in Madrid to persuade the Pope to send Campeggio. Well, didn't she?

HENRY. Perhaps.

ANNE. She did! She did! I know it.

HENRY (*aside*). Tomorrow I'll be hunting. Charging away, flying through the world, horses, dogs, men in pursuit of something that can actually be caught! (*To* ANNE.) Wolsey will work the bishops.

ANNE. Work Fisher? He hates me. No doubt he thinks I'm a demon goat. Or a witch. Or Martin Luther in woman's skirts…

HENRY. You've heard those things?

ANNE. Of course. Cooks in the kitchens up to your ministers in the Privy Chamber, they all whisper about me. Don't you think I know how palaces work?

HENRY. My love, I'm so sorry. I'll flog anyone… cook or earl…

ANNE. No one would dare say a word against me, if I were what you say you wish I were.

HENRY. Can't we just… be?

ANNE. Be what?

HENRY. Man and woman.

They look at each other.

ANNE. Just be.

HENRY. As in the song.

> 'To furnish forth our fate
> On some unhaunted isle
> Where harmless robin dwells with gentle thrush
> Happy we…

ANNE. Happy we…

HENRY. Obscure from all society
From love and hate and worldly foes…

ANNE. In contemplation spending all our days…
And loving ways to make us merry…

HENRY. Happy we…

ANNE. Happy we.'

A moment. Then they return to their real world.

You know what your wife will do. When, after delay after delay, the Court finally meets, she'll appear all innocent, calm, ill done by, full of godly airs, the perfect wife so infuriatingly in the right! And the bishops, piled up on their benches behind the Pope's man, will all burst into tears and nothing, nothing will be decided!

HENRY. The Court will work. It must work. There is nothing else.

ANNE. Nothing else?

HENRY. Wolsey warns that he can see no other way to get the Pope's approval.

ANNE. Oh, does he. Wolsey, Wolsey, woolly Wolsey…

HENRY. Anne…

ANNE (*whirling around*). Woolly woolly Wolsey, woolly sheep… butcher's son, let him butcher a sheep! Or, better, butcher him.

HENRY. He is my greatest servant! Be silent!

ANNE. He does look like a sheep.

HENRY. Stop it!

ANNE. Bah bah, bah bah.

HENRY. Anne…

ANNE. Bah bah, Wolsey black sheep… (*Pulls a face.*)

HENRY (*laughs*). Bah bah bah.

ANNE. Bah bah bah.

HENRY. Bah bah bah.

They laugh. HENRY *pulls her to him and they go to the ground. He puts his hand up her skirt.*

Allow me, further than your knee. After five years, Mistress, a little further than the knee?

ANNE. Yes, My Liege, Lord and Master, a little further.

HENRY. And… a view from behind?

ANNE. At a distance, with the curtain half closed.

> HENRY *stands and pulls her to her feet. They run hand in hand and exit.*

Scene Eight

Enter CROMWELL *and* SIMPKIN. *Enter* SLOOP *trying to overhear.*

CROMWELL. 'Gone?'

SIMPKIN. Slipped away.

CROMWELL. 'Slipped?'

SIMPKIN. Yes. Gone.

CROMWELL (*looks at a paper*). She's on the Court calendar as hunting with His Majesty. (*Slapping the paper.*) It says here, all day, with the hunt, then to Farnham Castle at sunset.

SIMPKIN. One of my men returned from the hunt, to say she is not with His Majesty.

CROMWELL (*screwing up the paper*). I've told you again and again! Make sure we know where everyone is, all the time! Who is talking to who, who is pissing on who, who is fucking who! (*Throws the paper at him.*) Who's with her?

SIMPKIN. She… may be alone.

CROMWELL. Alone?

SIMPKIN. Her palfrey was taken.

CROMWELL. No one else took a horse with her?

SIMPKIN. No one.

CROMWELL. You mean the King's mistress is out riding, alone? In the countryside? Amongst… *people*?

SIMPKIN. She said to the stable boy she would take the palfrey to water him. She is very fond of the animal.

CROMWELL. And she's an animal someone else is very fond of! I will personally administer whippings for this! Arses will be shredded! Get Rochford.

SIMPKIN. Yes, Sir Thomas. (*Turns to go.*)

CROMWELL. And Simpkin.

SIMPKIN. Sir Thomas?

CROMWELL. Don't let His Grace the Cardinal know. At least not from us. Not yet.

SIMPKIN. Sir Thomas.

SIMPKIN *goes.*

CROMWELL (*aside*). A court is like a rabbit warren. Many tunnels, but all in one hole. People must stay in the hole! They must not pop out!

He exits. SLOOP *waylays* SIMPKIN.

SLOOP. What game is she up to now?

SIMPKIN. Who?

SLOOP. The whore. She's gone off somewhere, hasn't she? Where? Has she got another lover?

SIMPKIN. How would I know?

He tries to get away. SLOOP *grabs him.*

SLOOP. How far, actually, has the King got with her? I mean… (*Gesture.*)

SIMPKIN. Do I stand at nights at the foot of the royal bed?

SLOOP. Come come, Simpkin, hasn't your master had a spyhole cut through the wall into the King's bedchamber?

SIMPKIN. Has he?

SLOOP. The carpenter was doing work in York House. He told me.

SIMPKIN. He could lose his tongue.

SLOOP. Surely you get a peep. In the dog hours.

SIMPKIN looks around.

SIMPKIN. She... (*Whispers in his ear.*)

SLOOP. Oooh. Really? Oooh. Interruptus ad infinitum.

LADY ROCHFORD passes. They bow to her, she ignores them. She goes away quickly. SIMPKIN runs after her.

SIMPKIN. My Lady Rochford...

They exit.

SLOOP (*aside*). The whole Court, tight. The King doesn't get his divorce from the Queen, doesn't get his end away with his tart. And we all... tighten. Intolerably. Five years of this. Something's going to have to snap.

He exits.

Scene Nine

Farnham Forest.

Enter ANNE.

ANNE. Anyone there? (*No one.*) I have left my horse... No one. (*Aside.*) The light. Just the upper branches of trees, moving a little. Birdsong. No voices. I am always surrounded by voices, in rooms, in halls, in corridors. Even when I lie down to sleep I hear the whispers of the people behind the spyholes, watching me. And in the open I ride with ladies and gentlemen, joshing, making courtly remarks, soldiers flanking us shouting orders. So suddenly to be alone... it's frightening. (*Shouts.*) Anyone?

Enter as if from nowhere four COUNTRY PEOPLE, poorly dressed. The MEN are armed. They stare at her.

I left my horse, by the stile just within the wood. Where the message said.

They continue to stare.

Well, will someone speak?

FIRST COUNTRY MAN (*Gloucestershire accent*). You really be her?

ANNE. 'Really be' who?

FIRST COUNTRY MAN. My Lady, please, this be more fraught to us than you can know.

FIRST COUNTRY WOMAN. You could be a creature of the Cardinal, sent to trap us.

ANNE. Yes, I know what the Cardinal is capable of. And the danger for all of us. (*Takes a glove from her hand. A ring.*) This ring was given me by His Majesty.

They hesitate.

Look.

The FIRST COUNTRY MAN *pushes the* SECOND COUNTRY WOMAN *forward. Timorously, she approaches* ANNE *and peers at the ring, not wanting to touch her hand. The great gulf between…*

Hold my hand, I am human.

The SECOND COUNTRY WOMAN *holds* ANNE*'s hand for a moment, looking very closely at the ring. Then she falls to her knees.*

SECOND COUNTRY WOMAN. My Lady.

The others bow.

OTHERS. My Lady.

ANNE. Take me to him, then.

SECOND COUNTRY MAN. This way, My Lady.

They lead her away and exit.

Scene Ten

CROMWELL, LADY ROCHFORD, SIMPKIN.

CROMWELL. My Lady Rochford.

ROCHFORD. Sir Thomas.

CROMWELL. Where is the Lady Anne?

ROCHFORD. She is… hunting with His Majesty.

CROMWELL. Oh, I think not.

ROCHFORD. Why, where else could she be, Sir Thomas?

CROMWELL. Don't be *bright* with me, Lady Rochford. They who are *bright* with me can find themselves suddenly dimmed. The Lady Anne and you are like giggling novices in a nunnery, sharing naughty thoughts behind the back of your Mother Superior. Though to see either of you as nuns stretches the imagination.

ROCHFORD. As does seeing you as a Mother Superior, Sir Thomas.

A nasty moment. Then CROMWELL *laughs.*

CROMWELL. So if she's not with the hunt…

ROCHFORD. The truth is, My Lady is indisposed.

CROMWELL. Nothing serious, I hope?

ROCHFORD. A slight head cold.

CROMWELL. *Quelle horreur!*

ROCHFORD. At the last moment she thought it best not to ride out today.

CROMWELL. With His Majesty's permission, of course.

ROCHFORD. Of course.

CROMWELL. So why didn't you tell me this at once?

A moment.

ROCHFORD. I was being too eager in my discretion. His Majesty is most concerned at the slightest sign of a cold. He is all too aware she once nearly died of the sweating sickness.

CROMWELL. He is loving in his concern. So she's sleeping now?

ROCHFORD. Yes.

CROMWELL. Excellent. Now tell me where she really is.

ROCHFORD. I…

CROMWELL. She's not in her chamber, sniffing cloves for a cold! She lied to the King! You helped her with that lie!

ROCHFORD. No.

CROMWELL. She was seen taking a horse! Did she think she wouldn't be seen? Did she think I don't have spies watching the stables, as I have spies everywhere? Don't you women know what world you're living in?

ROCHFORD. Oh, I think we know that, Sir Thomas.

CROMWELL. Where is she, you lying fucking bitch?

ROCHFORD (*shock*). Sir! I beg your pardon to be excused.

CROMWELL. Not granted.

ROCHFORD. I am withdrawing from this conversation.

CROMWELL. You are not, bitch!

ROCHFORD. Good day.

She turns to go. CROMWELL *nods to* SIMPKIN, *who grabs her arm. She pulls away.*

How dare you!

CROMWELL. Oh, dare dare, Simpkin, be *gallant*, dare all.

SIMPKIN lifts her up. She kicks and struggles, he throws her down in front of CROMWELL.

Who do you and the Boleyn woman think you are? Little girls, playing games? Do you think just because you're married to her brother you can do what you like? I can have you in the Tower, hung up, naked on a wall in chains, whipped by wires just like... (*Clicks his fingers.*) that! (*Close to her.*) She's gone to meet someone, hasn't she. Who is it?

ROCHFORD. Please, I promised!

CROMWELL. A lover?

ROCHFORD. No!

CROMWELL. Has she reverted to her true nature?

ROCHFORD. What?

CROMWELL. Whore! Whore! Is she whoring? Like she did at the French Court?

ROCHFORD. No! No!

CROMWELL. She has ridden out for a liaison, hasn't she! (*Closer.*) Tell me who with! Tell!

She whispers in his ear. He straightens, shocked.

Is she that... reckless?

He walks away and exits.

SIMPKIN *goes to help* LADY ROCHFORD. *She stands, withdrawing from him.*

SIMPKIN. My Lady.

He bows and moves away.

ROCHFORD. Oh to keep a secret at Court. Just one secret. That would be so beautiful. Anne, I'm so sorry, I told.

SIMPKIN. And you will again.

She turns on him. He bows and exits.

ROCHFORD (*aside*). It's the fear. It's like a big stone in the palm of your hand. That you must swallow. But how can you? How can you swallow that and not choke?

She exits.

Scene Eleven

Farnham Forest.

Enter ANNE *and the four* COUNTRY PEOPLE. *They bow and back away.*

Enter WILLIAM TYNDALE.

ANNE. Master William Tyndale?

TYNDALE (*Gloucestershire accent*). My Lady Boleyn?

A moment. Then he bows.

You sent a message to me, to where I was in Antwerp.

ANNE. Yes.

TYNDALE. Asking to meet me, if ever I came to England.

ANNE. Yes.

The COUNTRY PEOPLE *are uneasy.*

TYNDALE. My companions doubt your good faith.

FIRST COUNTRY WOMAN. The King's mistress with the likes of us, in a wood?

SECOND COUNTRY WOMAN. She's a creature from the Cardinal.

TYNDALE. Lady?

ANNE. We have a mutual friend in Christ. At the Court in France. He visited England with the French Ambassador, last year. He told me how to reach you.

TYNDALE. The Lord has his conspirators.

ANNE. Yes, doesn't he.

FIRST COUNTRY MAN. What be this Frenchman's name…

ANNE. Monsieur le Compte de…

TYNDALE (*interrupts*). No, no name! I love my country dear, but in these times I don't trust even the trees in England.

ANNE. We're rarely alone.

TYNDALE. No, we are not.

A flash of liking between them.

ANNE. I have heard the True Word.

TYNDALE. You? The King's… thing?

She flinches.

No no, I'm wrong to speak so. What you are is between you and your God. But I'll be frank: I find it hard to believe that you've heard the Word.

ANNE. 'The Lord worketh his purpose in strange ways.'

TYNDALE. True.

ANNE. Trust me, Master Tyndale.

TYNDALE. 'Trust.' (*A weary laugh.*) My Lady, I wrote the words of Christ's Gospel, so clear, so clean. But all has become dirty around me, phantasmagorical. I scuttle about Europe like a rat, hidey-hole to hidey-hole, in fear of the enemies of the Word.

ANNE. I don't think you are a man to fear anything, Master Tyndale. But, forgive me, you don't seem the scholar.

TYNDALE. No?

ANNE. Your speech is… unexpectedly rustic.

TYNDALE. 'Unexpectedly rustic?' (*Laughs*.)

ANNE. Forgive me, I'm being rude.

TYNDALE. Don't you fret, My Lady. Many say: how does this rough tongue get round six languages, translate the true Greek and Hebrew of Scripture into a Bible that makes the Pope himself shit in his sleep? (*Laughs*.) But they don't hear the Gloucestershire in my Bible. As they don't hear the Gospel's common word for the common man.

ANNE. Yes, that's right! Your speech is in your Testament.

TYNDALE. So you read my translation?

ANNE. Of course.

TYNDALE. It's a banned book, greatly burnt. Dangerous to have in the English Court, under the eyes of Cardinal Wolsey.

ANNE. His Grace the Cardinal doesn't see everything. There are many copies of your Testament at Court, behind walls, in secret panels.

TYNDALE. So the True Word is worming in the woodwork of English palaces? I praise the Lord.

ANNE. As I do.

TYNDALE. I'm thinking: is this a great wonder? Could God work His purpose through *you*?

ANNE. Through the Concubine, schooled in French ways?

TYNDALE. Now forgive my rudeness.

She smiles. He smiles.

ANNE. How can any of us know that we are God's instrument?

TYNDALE. We can't. But there's a good rule of thumb: they who claim to be God's instrument, never are. You do what you do, and stand in faith, and hope.

ANNE. As Martin says.

TYNDALE. Yes. Extraordinary to hear you say that name.

ANNE. In my world I never can say it. How wonderful it is to stand here, in this wood, and say: Martin Luther.

TYNDALE. Martin Luther.

ANNE, turning wildly, shouting up at the trees.

ANNE. Martin Luther! Martin Luther! Martin Luther!

Unease amongst his companions.

FIRST COUNTRY WOMAN. Master William…

TYNDALE. What is it you want, Lady Anne?

ANNE. To read your new book.

The COUNTRY PEOPLE *are incredulous.*

TYNDALE. You've heard of my new book?

ANNE. Yes, from the Cardinal.

Unease again from the COUNTRY PEOPLE.

He told me it was the work of an extremist, heretical beyond all reason, from a pen in the service of the Antichrist.

TYNDALE. The work has its critics.

ANNE. He's only heard of it, not read it.

TYNDALE. A true critic then. (*To the* FIRST COUNTRY MAN.) Give her a copy of the book.

FIRST COUNTRY MAN. She'll give it to the Cardinal for him to burn!

TYNDALE. I don't think so.

The FIRST COUNTRY MAN *takes a book from a bag and, reluctantly, hands it to* ANNE.

ANNE. Thank you, Master Tyndale.

TYNDALE. A book won't break the Pope's power in England. That will take a King.

ANNE *stares at him, then turns to go.*

ANNE. Good day, Master Tyndale.

TYNDALE. Sing Martin's hymn with us.

She turns back.

The FIRST COUNTRY WOMAN *steps forward and sings the first line of the last verse of 'A Mighty Fortress is Our God'.*

FIRST COUNTRY WOMAN (*singing*).
    God's Word above…

ANNE.…all earthly powers.

ALL (*singing*).
    No thanks to them, abideth;
    The Spirit and the gifts are ours,
    Through Him who with us sideth.
    Let good and loved ones go,
    This mortal life also;
    The body they may kill;
    God's Truth abideth still;
    His Kingdom is for ever.

TYNDALE *and the* COUNTRY PEOPLE *exit.* ANNE *stands for a moment with the book. She opens it slowly. She reads. She snaps it shut. Then she holds up the book to the sky and closes her eyes in prayer.*

ANNE. Lord Jesus. By Your Divine Will, You have put this sword into my hand. Now give me Your Grace to use it well. Amen.

She exits, quickly.

Scene Twelve

Enter LADY ROCHFORD, JANE *and* CELIA. LADY
ROCHFORD *is reading* The Obedience of a Christian Man.
JANE *and* CELIA *run to her.*

LADY ROCHFORD *gasps and closes the book.*

JANE. My Lady, what's that?

CELIA. Is it a Lancelot story? The knight, coming out of the
lake, naked in the dawn...

JANE.... Queen Guinevere, lying on the mossy bank...

CELIA.... Wearing nothing but her long hair...

They laugh.

ROCHFORD. No. Nothing like that.

*She shoos them away, walks and carries on reading. They
follow her. They remain on the stage.*

Enter SLOOP *and* SIMPKIN.

SLOOP *vomits.*

SIMPKIN. What's the matter?

SLOOP. I've just been on an errand for His Grace the Cardinal.

SIMPKIN. What? Tasting oysters?

SLOOP. His Grace does like his Colchester natives. No. He sent
me to Sir Thomas More's house.

SIMPKIN. And Sir Thomas poisoned you?

SLOOP. He's torturing a Protestant in his basement. He insisted
I see. Took me down there. He's got his very own private
dungeon! And was very pleased with a new rack he's had
sent from Holland. It's portable.

SIMPKIN. A portable rack. Very handy. You're travelling, you're at an inn, a man begins to annoy you…

SLOOP. The Prot was on the machine. It's called the Dutchman's Daughter. It sort of stretches you and at the same time folds you up.

SIMPKIN. Yes, that would sort out your theological views…

SLOOP. I mean, I've been to executions for a day out with the wife, hangings and brandings, but this… In that small room, this was… His gut had split. Down his side. And he was screaming.

SIMPKIN. Not surprising…

SLOOP. No, you don't get it. He was screaming the name of our Lord.

They look at each other.

What is it about religion?

SIMPKIN. Ask questions like that and you're on the way to the rack yourself.

Another part of the stage. SLOOP *and* SIMPKIN *notice* LADY ROCHFORD *and the excitement over the book.*

ROCHFORD. All right. All right. (*Hands the book to* JANE.) But Lady Anne will expect me to return it by this evening. Keep it close.

JANE. We will, My Lady.

Exit LADY ROCHFORD.

JANE *and* CELIA *huddle over the book.*

CELIA. Oh. Look what it says there, about His Holiness the Pope. Lady Anne is reading *this*?

JANE. Let's give it back, now…

But SLOOP *and* SIMPKIN *waylay them.*

SIMPKIN. And what are we reading that's so exciting, my ladies?

JANE. Nothing, sir…

SLOOP. A sweet nothing?

SIMPKIN. Steamy sweet nothing?

SLOOP. Give it here.

JANE. No!

> *They are boisterous.* SLOOP *grabs the book.* SIMPKIN *pushes* JANE *off him.* CELIA *steps back, appalled.*

> SLOOP *opens the book and looks at the title page.*

CELIA. I've not read it, I haven't, really, I haven't… (*Holds her face.*)

> *For a moment they are all still.*

> *Then a shocked* SLOOP *holds the book out to* SIMPKIN.

> SIMPKIN *stares at it then at* JANE *and* CELIA.

> LADY ROCHFORD *enters, sees the scene and rushes to them.*

ROCHFORD. Give me that!

SLOOP. Oh, I think not, My Lady.

ROCHFORD. Give it!

SLOOP. Oooh ooh ooh, no no. I think His Grace the Cardinal must see this.

ROCHFORD. His Grace, why?

SLOOP. He's had us searching the Court for heretical books, in cupboards, under cushions, floorboards, up chimneys. Oh, he'll be so merry to see this, he'll dance up and down, his little feet will go twiddle twiddle. He's got little feet, you know. For so heavy a man. So frightening a man.

ROCHFORD. Don't tell His Grace.

SLOOP. No? What would persuade my friend and me not to tell? What favour could you possibly offer us, My Lady Rochford? (*Indicating* JANE *and* CELIA.) One of these?

ROCHFORD. Damn you, creature.

SIMPKIN. I think… just take the book.

SLOOP. Oh, I'll take the book to His Grace. And you. Come!

ROCHFORD. Make me!

SLOOP. Do you really want me to do that, My Lady?

A moment.

ROCHFORD (*to* JANE, *quickly*). Go. Tell Lady Anne what has happened.

JANE turns to leave.

SLOOP. Stop!

JANE stops.

And where is she going?

ROCHFORD. Errr… Shirts. We have to deliver shirts to His Majesty. Sewn by Lady Anne.

SLOOP. Touching.

SIMPKIN. Doesn't the Queen sew the King's shirts?

ROCHFORD. They both do.

SLOOP. Competitive shirt-making?

SIMPKIN. That's what happens when sex 'n' politics get mixed up.

SLOOP. Loads of shirts for the man.

SIMPKIN and SLOOP laugh.

(*To* JANE.) Go on then! Take His Majesty his linen. You two, come!

Exit JANE.

Scene Thirteen

WOLSEY *and* CROMWELL *enter to join* LADY ROCHFORD *and* CELIA – *who is in tears* – *and* SLOOP *and* SIMPKIN.

SLOOP *hands the book to* WOLSEY, *who opens it, flicks through a few pages, then quietly closes it and hands it to* CROMWELL, *who glances at it and sighs.* WOLSEY *takes it from him.*

WOLSEY. All right. All right. All will be well. All, well. (*A moment.*) Where did you get it?

ROCHFORD. I am not at liberty to say.

WOLSEY. Oh, you are not at liberty in anything, My Lady, no no. How dare you presume you are! Only one has liberty, and that is His Majesty, we are all utterly disposable to him, are we not! As he is disposable to Almighty God!

ROCHFORD. Yes, Your Grace.

WOLSEY. So who gave you the book?

ROCHFORD. I found it.

WOLSEY. Really? Where? Was it lying around in some privy, for light reading?

ROCHFORD. It was on a settle.

WOLSEY. Oh, on a settle! Just... there for all to see. To pick up. The most notorious, reviled, condemned, banned and damned book in Christendom!

CROMWELL. It was perhaps simply discarded, Your Grace. By someone in fear of being found with it.

ROCHFORD. Yes, Your Grace, it was on a window seat, I picked it up, I thought it was, perhaps, a romance. Arthur.

Round Table. Knights. In armour. With strong arms.
Maidens. With white arms.

CROMWELL. You see, what would a woman of the Court have
to do with theology?

WOLSEY. Ah. Ah. (*A moment.*) But you said you found it on a
settle.

ROCHFORD. Did I?

WOLSEY. Well, which was it, settle or window seat?

ROCHFORD. I…

WOLSEY. No, there's conspiracy here. I try to purge this Court
of filthy heretical writing, but still it bubbles up! Like
sewage from the Devil's drains. Is there a cabal of you?
Passing around filthy materials? To read in secret corners, up
against the Palace walls, in night-time orchards, fornicating
with heresy like Martin Luther's whores?

ROCHFORD. No no…

WOLSEY. What if I send you along the river, to Sir Thomas
More's house? (*Wagging the book.*) He specialises in this
kind of thing. Yes, you will have a little talk with Sir Thomas.

ROCHFORD. No, please, please…

WOLSEY. Sloop, arrange for a boat to go to Chelsea.

ROCHFORD. No!

WOLSEY. Tell me who gave you the book!

ROCHFORD. I… It… I…

Enter ANNE, *followed by* JANE. ANNE *sweeps up to*
WOLSEY.

ANNE. You have my book, Your Grace. Please return it.

She holds out her hand. A silence, all dead still.

WOLSEY. Lady Rochford, you and your women, please leave
us. (*Holds out his hand.*)

LADY ROCHFORD *looks to* ANNE, *who nods her approval.*

ROCHFORD. Your Grace. (*Curtsies. Kisses his hand.*)

WOLSEY (*close to her*). You have come close to fire, you know that?

ROCHFORD. Th… thank you, Your Grace.

CELIA. Your Grace. (*Curtsies, kisses his hand.*)

JANE. Your Grace. (*Curtsies, kisses his hand.*)

LADY ROCHFORD, CELIA *and* JANE *exit.* LADY ROCHFORD *sneaks back to try to listen.*

WOLSEY. Your book?

ANNE. Yes. Return it.

WOLSEY. What are you, madam?

ANNE. I am your next Queen.

The MEN *present are startled.*

WOLSEY. Madam, in your remarks, be advised to keep to good form.

ANNE. 'Good form'? Oh yes, we must have 'good form'. You work day and night to find a way His Majesty can divorce that woman from Aragon. And marry the future Queen, the Queen of his heart. Me. But we must not say that because of 'form'.

WOLSEY. His Majesty, sadly, because of certain passages of Holy Scripture, feels his conscience dictates that he must divorce his wife. But whether he marries you is not a scriptural matter. Nor one of conscience. More of lust.

ANNE. Now you offend 'good form'…

WOLSEY. Lust! Inflamed, perhaps, by practices.

ANNE. 'Practices'?

WOLSEY. There is still, on Earth, a decayed old religion. Christ by his birth drove it into dark corners, where it lives on in the minds of ignorant women.

ANNE. Your Grace, are you accusing me of witchcraft?

WOLSEY. I am asking: what are you?

ANNE. Fertile. (*A moment.*) I am fertile! Are you? (*Laughs.*) What a pity you don't have a womb, Cardinal. Then *you* could give the King a son and heir!

WOLSEY. How dare you!

ANNE. Give me my book.

WOLSEY. I will not. It is heretical. I will tell the King you had it.

ANNE. Telltale all you want.

WOLSEY. Need I remind you how hotly the King wrote as Defender of the Faith, against Luther and the Protestants?

ANNE. In the past, yes. Though Sir Thomas More wrote most of that book, and wasn't it your idea anyway?

WOLSEY. God may have had me prompt the royal quill...

ANNE (*interrupting*). Phoo phoo! You wanted an alliance with Spain. And a certain marriage with Aragon. But oh, look, all has changed: is His Majesty's policy still to favour Spain? No. And is he still in love with the woman from Aragon? The cow who cannot litter?

WOLSEY. You are foul, madam!

ANNE. I am driven to it by foul men!

WOLSEY. You will not marry him. You are not royal. You are a schemer, a plotter, an adventuress! Well, we've had those at Court before. But you are more dangerous. I have long suspected you to be infected with bad religion. And now I know you are, madam: you stink of it, you drip with the syphilis of Luther's teaching! (*Waggles book.*) This is the proof!

ANNE. You once blocked a marriage of mine. You will not do so again, Your Grace.

WOLSEY. We shall see. Good day, Lady Anne.

He turns away, followed by SLOOP. *Just before he exits he jumps in the air, twiddling his feet.*

CROMWELL *and* SIMPKIN *exit.*

ANNE (*aside*). Why do they hate the idea of a woman standing naked before her God? (*Pacing.*) I shouldn't have said that about Catherine, I shouldn't, I shouldn't, I should be demure and neat, eyes down, book of Holy Hours in my hands. But I want... I want... (*Aside again.*) I want the King. In me. His child in me. And our child born into a new world. And Catherine *is*... such a cow! (*Stamps her foot.*)

LADY ROCHFORD, JANE *and* CELIA *rush to* ANNE. ANNE *pushes them aside.*

ROCHFORD. My Lady, forgive me, I gave the book to Celia and the Cardinal's man came up on her...

CELIA. I'm so sorry, so sorry...

ANNE *flicks her hand at them.*

JANE. What will the Cardinal do?

ANNE. What do you think? His worst. (*Paces.*)

CELIA. Oh no, no... (*Crosses herself.*) *Salve, Regina...*

CELIA / JANE (*joining in, out of sync*).

Salve, Regina, Mater misericordiae, Vita,

Dulcedo, et spes nostra, salve...

ANNE. Stop that! Stop it! (*To* LADY ROCHFORD.) All of you, go to the chapel and pray. If anything happens, be found there. Not with me.

ROCHFORD. Anne...

ANNE. Go!

Exit LADY ROCHFORD, CELIA *and* JANE, *quickly.*

Scene Fourteen

CROMWELL *comes forward,* SIMPKIN *at a distance.* SLOOP *enters and tries to overhear.*

ANNE. The book, the Cardinal's got the book. The book the book. The Cardinal's got the book. He'll burn it, burn me with it. Oh, what to do what to do!

CROMWELL. My Lady Anne.

ANNE. Master Cromwell.

    CROMWELL *turns and sees* SLOOP, *who backs away.*

CROMWELL. Shall we walk in the orchard? It's a very fine night.

ANNE. Walk alone?

CROMWELL. Why not? Do you fear me?

ANNE. Yes. You are the Cardinal's man.

CROMWELL. Am I?

    A moment.

    The orchard? There are perhaps holes for worms in apples. But none for spies.

    ANNE *hesitates for a moment. They turn on the stage and are handed lanterns.* CROMWELL *acquires an apple.*

    They are now walking in an orchard.

    I know who gave you that sinful, sinful book.

    She stops.

    Is Master Tyndale well?

ANNE. How did you...?

CROMWELL....know you met him? Ah.

ANNE. You forced Jane Rochford to tell, didn't you.

CROMWELL. Of course.

ANNE. How dare you bully one of my friends!

CROMWELL. How dare *you* tell a woman like that you were going to do something so sensitive. Lady Rochford is one of the world's leakers. Master Tyndale could have been betrayed. But he's on his way back to Holland now. He'll be safe, thanks to the Lord's guiding hand.

    CROMWELL *bites the apple.* ANNE *stares at him.*

ANNE. You are protecting Master Tyndale?

CROMWELL. Yes.

ANNE. You... arranged for him to come into the country?

CROMWELL. Yes.

ANNE. Did he know you did?

CROMWELL. Certainly not. If he had been caught, I couldn't have his presence laid at my door. But I... eased his passage.

ANNE. Why did you do that?

CROMWELL. Why do you think?

ANNE. You believe in the Word?

    He smiles.

    (*Lower.*) You are a Protestant?

CROMWELL. As I suspect you are, Lady Anne. (*A moment.*) You have my life in your hands.

    CROMWELL *bites the apple.*

ANNE. You have mine in yours.

CROMWELL. Yes. We are at a balance.

    CROMWELL *bites the apple. A pause. Then* ANNE *laughs.*

ANNE. They see you as a vicious man on the make.

CROMWELL. They see you as a hussy who planned to get your claws into the King from the moment you came to Court.

CROMWELL bites the apple. ANNE *looks at him calmly.*

ANNE. Let us say we are both creatures of this world.

CROMWELL. While being servants of another.

A pause.

ANNE. The Cardinal will go to the King, say terrible things about Master Tyndale's book, blast me as a heretic who has ensnared him…

CROMWELL (*laughs*). You are a heretic, you have ensnared him.

ANNE. Don't you understand? I have gone headlong, these years. Headlong. Everything has come to me. But for the first time I'm… frightened.

CROMWELL. I learnt as a boy: when you know someone's going to hit you, hit them first. When I was big enough, I tried it on my father. It worked. Go to the King, now, tonight. Wolsey will be having his dinner, he always stuffs himself before he politicks.

ANNE. Yes. Yes. I'll go…

CROMWELL. Though take a moment with me.

ANNE hesitates.

You know Martin Luther's evening prayer?

ANNE. Yes.

They hold their hands out, looking up – not kneeling. They take alternate lines until the last.

My Heavenly Father, I thank You, through Jesus Christ, your beloved Son, that you have protected me by Your Grace…

CROMWELL. … Forgive, I pray, all my sins and the evil I have done…

ANNE. ... Protect me, by Your Grace, tonight...

CROMWELL / ANNE. I put myself in Your care, body and soul and all that I have. Be with me, Lord, so that the evil enemy will not gain power over me. Amen.

CROMWELL. Good. Let's go and tear down a Cardinal.

CROMWELL *exits.* ANNE *stays onstage for...*

Scene Fifteen

Enter HENRY. *Enter lurking* COURTIERS.

HENRY. At your devotions?

ANNE. Yes.

HENRY. And he snatched it from you?

ANNE. Yes.

HENRY. While you were kneeling, praying? He snatched your prayer book from you? I won't have this! (*To a* COURTIER.) Get the Cardinal Wolsey from his dinner, now.

The COURTIER *rushes off.*

What, was the book valuable? Illustrated, gold leaf, that he envied?

ANNE. Not exactly.

HENRY. His greed outstrips his sense. He eats, he piles up houses, horses, land, rare books and does nothing for my great matter! Now he spends time frightening you, my sweet.

ANNE. It wasn't a prayer book.

HENRY. A Gospel? Worse! To tear Holy Scripture from a kneeling woman's hands? (*Shouts off.*) Get that fat man here!

ANNE. The book was written by William Tyndale.

A pause.

HENRY. My love, did you say…

ANNE. The book is by William Tyndale. It is called *The Obedience of a Christian Man.*

HENRY. Sweet heart of mine, that is… that is a book that is proscribed. On a list that I proscribed.

ANNE. Drawn up by His Grace the Cardinal.

HENRY. Yes, but all the same, William Tyndale is… The man is close to Luther.

ANNE. It is a most sensible book. Which the Cardinal banned for a reason.

HENRY. Many reasons, I imagine.

ANNE. But one above all. It argues that kings are responsible directly to God. Not to the Pope.

HENRY. How does it argue that?

ANNE. From Scripture.

HENRY. Argues that from Scripture?

ANNE. Master Tyndale writes that England should be an independent, sovereign nation state, under God but no longer under the power of the Pope.

HENRY. Independent… sovereign… state. But what of the Church?

ANNE. God anointed Your Majesty King. Therefore it is His Will that you be Head of His Church.

HENRY. This is in Scripture?

ANNE. Yes, My Lord. The book exposes the falsity of all prelates and popes, arguing directly from God's Word. (*Curtsies low to him and stays down.*)

HENRY. But if I *were* Head of the Church of England, to whom would I appeal for my divorce? (*Laughs*.) To myself?

ANNE is silent and still. He realises the full import of the argument and stares at her. She is looking down.

ANNE. My Sovereign Lord, it is the way to all your desires.

HENRY (*pauses, wags his finger at her, slowly*). You, you... think dangerously.

Enter WOLSEY followed by CROMWELL, SLOOP and SIMPKIN, LADY ROCHFORD and COURTIERS.

WOLSEY is holding the book up. He sees ANNE bowed and hesitates for a moment.

WOLSEY. Your Majesty, it grieves me to report a most heinous, offensive matter, sadly implicating the Lady Anne. This book...

HENRY. Return it.

WOLSEY. What?

HENRY. Return the book to Lady Anne.

WOLSEY. Sire, it is heretical...

HENRY. No, Your Grace. From what I hear it is a book for all kings and for me to read.

CROMWELL smiles.

HENRY holds out his hand to ANNE. She takes it and stands.

So. Give her the book.

WOLSEY. Your Majesty, I protest.

HENRY. Protest? What do you protest? That you have not had enough dinner? Very well, make up for it at breakfast.

HENRY frowns at WOLSEY. Sniggers amongst the COURTIERS. CROMWELL and ANNE exchange a glance.

All but WOLSEY *exit.*

WOLSEY (*aside*). Where did that anger come from? Suddenly. Ruin in his eyes. Suddenly… I feel all my greatness flowing from me. Summer, you're in the sumptuous robes of power, then… the blink of an eye and it's winter, and you're naked in the frost. No, I won't have it. I won't slip away, lamenting the whims of princes! I won't go quietly, meditating on man's rise and fall, whingeing about fate and wanton boys, pulling off the wings of flies. I'll not fall like Lucifer, never to hope again. I'll fight. (*A moment.*) Fight. (*A moment.*) Fight.

Enter CROMWELL *with* SLOOP *and* SIMPKIN.

CROMWELL. His Majesty requests that you do not return to York House tonight. There is a barge waiting to take you to Richmond.

WOLSEY. Cromwell, what…

CROMWELL. It's nothing, Your Grace. His Majesty merely wishes me to search your home for papers.

WOLSEY. What papers?

CROMWELL. Secret letters between you and the Pope. Frustrating His Majesty's wishes in the matter of his divorce.

WOLSEY. There are no such letters!

CROMWELL. Then I won't find them, will I.

They all exit.

Scene Sixteen

Enter HENRY *and* ANNE. SERVANTS *lurk. Musicians play.*

ANNE (*aside*). In Calais. Two years later.

> HENRY *and* ANNE *rush to each other and embrace. He whirls her around.* SERVANTS *give them wine goblets. They raise them.*

The King of France!

HENRY. The King of France!

ANNE. The King of France!

HENRY. What is the matter with his mouth?

ANNE. His mouth is perfect, he is a king.

HENRY. It's all skew-whiff.

ANNE. It is perhaps the French breeding of cousins with cousins?

HENRY. But the spitting!

ANNE. He was friendly.

HENRY. Yes!

ANNE. It was a triumph.

HENRY. When you held private conference with him, what did he say?

ANNE. That he wished to see us married.

HENRY. He said that?

ANNE. He has alliances with the Pope he cannot defy, but will do everything to help us.

HENRY. He said that. Through the spitting.

ANNE. Yes.

HENRY. Francis was courteous to you?

ANNE. He treated me… royally.

HENRY. Royally.

ANNE. Yes.

HENRY. As he should.

ANNE. My Lord…

HENRY. His support will be implicit, though, not open…

ANNE. My Lord…

HENRY. The trick will be to make it known that he supports our marrying.

ANNE. My Lord…

HENRY. The more it is known amongst the Courts of Europe, the more pressure there will be on the Pope…

ANNE. My Lord…

HENRY. The Holy See is weak, alliances go both ways, he will have to accept a marriage…

ANNE. Henry.

HENRY. What? (*Looks at her.*) Oh. Anne?

ANNE. Seven years is long enough to have waited, don't you think?

HENRY. Yes. I have longed…

ANNE. I too.

HENRY. Why… why now?

ANNE. Why not?

HENRY. Little cat.

ANNE. Big bull.

HENRY. Cat and bull? (*Laughs.*)

ANNE. True love.

HENRY. Wife to me.

They touch. They are sliding into an embrace. They break away, still holding hands.

ANNE. Ladies and Gentlemen. There will now be a fifteen-minute interval.

End of Act One.

ACT TWO

Scene One

Musicians playing. Enter JAMES *wearing* ANNE*'s coronation dress, hand in hand with* GEORGE, *who is not in drag. They dance as man and woman, beautifully, arms extended, whirling figures. The music stops, they embrace and kiss passionately.*

GEORGE (*aside*). Well, it's something different. And if you're going to advance, you find you have to swim in strange waters. Not unpleasant, really.

He returns to the passionate kiss.

Enter CECIL, *carrying a pile of books and papers. He is followed by* PARROT. SERVANTS *enter and hold back.*

CECIL (*shocked*). Your Majesty…

JAMES *still has* GEORGE *in his arms.*

JAMES. What?

CECIL. The bishops and the divines are assembling.

JAMES. They are doing what?

CECIL. Assembling.

JAMES. What is that, some lewd practice? (*To* GEORGE.) An assemblage of bishops and divines, assembling dissembled robes with secret hands.

He gooses GEORGE – *who yelps – and lets him go.*

Oh, Steamy. We always knew the fun and kissing would have to stop. Now the politicking begins. Steamy, be discreet.

GEORGE (*low, but loud enough to be heard*). Yes, my love.

CECIL (*aside*). Thank the good Lord for that.

JAMES (*to* SERVANTS). Get me out of this whore's dress!

>   SERVANTS *rush forward and begin to help him out of the dress.*

>   I will sit upon a chair, the velvet chair, I think – yes yes yes. You can win an argument by the way you place yourself in a room. And no benches! They'll stand. Let rheumatic knees cut theology short.

>   CECIL *gestures to two* SERVANTS, *who exit, running.*

CECIL. I am sure the bishops and divines will comply happily with Your Majesty's wishes.

JAMES. I'm not. Not not, oh no. Why? I am attempting to reform the Church of England. (*This while skirts are being pulled up over his head.*) To settle the religious argy-bargy, tupping and tipping and nonsense, once and for all. For the quiet and peace of this slimy, fractious, devious realm. (*Head appears.*) There will be knocked heads, Baron Cecil! Knocked heads.

CECIL. As long as there are not cut ones. Ha!

>   JAMES *does not laugh. Glares. Nasty moment.*

JAMES. Do not count on it. We all know religion can kill. (*Now in underwear.*) It is so so so so so so… cold. My balls are hard as peas.

>   SERVANTS *rush forward with clothes for the* KING *and help him into them.*

>   Master Parrot. Is the Thames still frozen this morning?

PARROT. Yes, Your Majesty. They say the ice is more than a foot thick.

JAMES. And are there puppet shows, and bulls being baited and interludes, and food cooking and lewd tippling, is it all a carnival, a Bacchanalian triumph…?

PARROT. Yes, Your Majesty. There is a fair on the ice.

JAMES. Then, Robert, I will hold the meeting there. Let fat bishops skate about, falling on their behinds, arguing the meanwhile about the nature of baptism. To the ice with religious dispute!

CECIL. I do not think that practical, Your Majesty.

JAMES. Robert, you have the most literal mind. Have you no sense of the fantastical?

CECIL. None at all, Sire. That is why I am so effective in this fantastical world.

JAMES. Ah. Ah. Ah. Was that wit, Robert?

CECIL. No, Sire.

PARROT. There are…

CECIL. Be quiet.

JAMES. No, Master Parrot, what? Speak, Parrot. Ha ha!

CECIL. Droll, Your Majesty. (*Gestures to* PARROT*: 'Speak'*.)

PARROT. Nothing, Sire.

JAMES. What, not a squawk?

JAMES *finishing his dressing*.

PARROT (*aside*). They don't know what it's like out there. Thieves like flies on the ice all year round.

JAMES. I am thinking of putting new laws through Parliament against thieves on the ice all year round. What do you think, Master Parrot?

PARROT (*mouth open*). I…

JAMES. Worth a squawk?

PARROT. Yes, Sire! Excellent, Sire! (*Aside*.) Do they read your very thoughts in Scotland?

Enter the two SERVANTS *with the velvet chair. They set it down.*

JAMES. A little further here.

They move the chair.

At a meeting with fractious men, always sit with your back to the light of a window. They can't see your eyes, but you can see theirs. Now for bishops and bigots! Dean Lancelot Andrewes I know. Who leads the Puritans?

CECIL. Doctor John Reynolds. I have intelligence on him here… (*Offering papers.*)

JAMES (*waving the papers away*). Dean of Lincoln, scholar of Queen's College, Oxford. Admonished once by Her late Majesty: Elizabeth accused him of devious fracticiousness. See, I have done my study. Is he wild?

CECIL. There are wilder.

JAMES. Amongst his party?

CECIL. There is a man called Henry Barrow.

JAMES. Huh. A lunatic at a meeting can be an advantage. Everyone unites against him. (*Sits.*) Bring in Andrewes and his Anglicans first. I will soften them a little. Or soften up. Ha!

CECIL (*to a* SERVANT). Now.

The SERVANT *exits.*

A black look from CECIL.

JAMES. Have no dark thoughts towards George Villiers, Robert. He is my sweet child and wife.

CECIL. Yes, Your Majesty. (*Sighs.*)

Enter DEAN LANCELOT ANDREWES *of Westminster Abbey, with* DIVINES. *They kneel.*

JAMES. Your Graces, gentlemen. It pleases me to thank Almighty God for bringing me into a promised land, this England, where religion is purely professed. I find I sit amongst grave, learned and reverend men. Please.

He gestures to them to rise and they do.

Dean Andrewes, speak to me of the state of the Church of England.

ANDREWES. Your Majesty, the Church of England has stood in a near-perfect state, like the primitive Church of our Lord, these past forty years. Indeed…

JAMES (*interrupts*). Forty years? Pis h posh! Ha! Just because a man's been sick of the pox for forty years, does that mean he shouldn't be cured?

ANDREWES. Your Majesty…

JAMES. Doesn't everything in this world decay and decline? Why not an institution? No. My Church will reform. *My* Church, Your Graces, Your Divinities! I am Head of the Church of England. First, understand this: you are not to persecute Puritans.

Horror among the DIVINES.

I know that, in Her late Majesty's reign, some amongst you treated them brutally. I will have no more rackings, brandings and burnings, no persecution!

ANDREWES. Your Majesty, why are you playing the Puritan?

JAMES. Because, Dean, I am your King Solomon. I can play any which way I choose. Now, who will play the baby, which Solomon ordered cut in half?

Some laugh but there is unease.

For isn't that what you'd do to my Church? Cut it in half?

ANDREWES. What of Catholics?

A rustle among the DIVINES.

JAMES (*smiles*). What? Are there some here, disguised in the priestly frocks of Church of England vicars? Polishing their altar rails, swinging, perhaps, a little too much incense on a Sunday? (*Smile goes.*) Catholics who fled abroad are welcome to return.

Discontent among the DIVINES.

ANDREWES. Sire, Roman Catholics are the enemies of your throne!

JAMES. Oh dear, oh dear. (*Slaps his hand.*) Naughty naughty. I have talked to the Jesuits.

ANDREWES. Your Majesty has talked to...

JAMES. They unmasked a Catholic plot against me. The criminals have been arrested. But all loyal Catholics have my protection.

Uproar among the DIVINES.

ANDREWES. Sire, you played the Puritan, now you play the Papist!

JAMES. Understand, Dean. I am for the medium in all things. I will have a new way in my Kingdom, in which all are included. You will be moderate or I'll damn well have you all strung up in chains in the Fleet Prison!

ANDREWES *and the* DIVINES *recoil.*

Bring in the other religionists.

CECIL. Now!

Enter JOHN REYNOLDS, HENRY BARROW *just behind him, and other* PURITANS. *They kneel.* JAMES *gestures for them to get up.*

JAMES. Doctor Reynolds. I am now ready to hear, at large, what you can object or say to the Church of England.

REYNOLDS. The sacraments of the Church must be reformed.

ANDREWES. There has been reform enough to the Church of England.

REYNOLDS. Not so.

ANDREWES. Very much so.

CECIL (*aside*). Five hours later.

All rearrange into exhausted disarray. JAMES *appears to be asleep.*

REYNOLDS. Baptism should not be for babies!

ANDREWES. False! All the ancient fathers baptised the very young!

REYNOLDS. Baptism in the Scriptures is for adults! Who come to Jesus by their free will!

ANDREWES. Infant souls are saved from Hell by baptism. One early father saved the soul of a dying child by baptising him with sand.

JAMES (*suddenly awake*). Sand? Baptised by sand? A turd for that argument. He might as well have pissed on the bairn, that would have been more like water than sand.

The ANGLICANS *are appalled, the* PURITANS *laugh.*

But as for myself, I am grateful for anything that will keep me from hellfire.

The ANGLICANS *like that, the* PURITANS *do not.*

Come on come on, keep going! No dinner until you've done!

REYNOLDS. I… I do not like the marriage ceremony.

JAMES. Is it the ceremony you dislike or the wife it gave to you?

REYNOLDS. I am not married, Your Majesty.

JAMES. Oop, oop whoops, oh dear. Well, some speak of Robin Hood who never shot his bow.

GEORGE *suddenly laughs at this.* JAMES *glances at him.*

What do you object to in the ceremony?

REYNOLDS. The words 'with my body I thee worship'.

JAMES. If you had a wife, you'd find you'd want to worship her, and fire all the arrows you could. Ha! What is the matter between you Puritans and bodies?

BARROW. Your Majesty! We do not come to the nub!

JAMES. What knob, sir?

BARROW. Nub, Sire!

JAMES leans to CECIL.

CECIL. Henry Barrow.

JAMES. Master Barrow. Hasten to your nub.

BARROW. The power of bishops!

Here it comes… they all concentrate.

Where in the Gospels are there bishops?

ANDREWES. Sir, the Apostles were the first bishops!

BARROW. The Apostles were godly men who preached God's Word! They wore no fancy hats, long surplices of gold, gold crosses, rings on fat fingers. They were rough-hewn, common men, bringing the Word to the people!

ANDREWES. What, then, would you have instead of bishops?

BARROW. The Word of God. The Lord is my shepherd, not the Bishop of such-and-such or this-and-this. The Word of God can come through any man.

ANDREWES. Especially through you.

BARROW. Through any man.

ANDREWES. What, are you an Apostle?

BARROW. No. But I have the spirit of the Apostles.

ANDREWES. The spirit of the Apostles is in you? Of Peter, James, Paul, in you?

BARROW. Yes, the spirit of the Apostles!

ANDREWES. How much?

BARROW. What?

ANDREWES. How much of this spirit is in your… person?

BARROW. As much as God has seen fit to pour into me!

ANDREWES. As much as there is in, say… St Paul?

BARROW. No, not as much! But it is the same spirit, there is but one spirit.

REYNOLDS. I think…

ANDREWES. Master Barrow, what Church Government would you have?

A moment. Even BARROW *is aware they are now on dangerous ground.*

BARROW. Let the faithful rule themselves.

ANDREWES. How?

REYNOLDS. Your Majesty.

He is increasingly uneasy.

BARROW. Let congregations choose their own ministers and pastors.

ANDREWES. So you would have a Church run by lowly ministers and pastors. Responsible not to any higher authority but their congregations.

BARROW. And the Word of God!

ANDREWES. And what is that kind of Church Government called?

CECIL (*aside*). At last the word is in the room. (*Looks at a corner of the stage.*) There it is: big, black and monstrous, elephant-size, a great trunk, claws, red eyes. Even I can see it and I have no imagination. And who will say the word first?

JAMES. Presbyterianism! (*Looks at the same corner of the stage as* CECIL *did.*) Yes, there it is. Ha!

REYNOLDS. Perhaps… the bishops could govern jointly with a presbytery of their brethren ministers and pastors of the Church…

JAMES. If you aim at a Scots presbytery, I tell you it agrees with a monarch as much as God agrees with the Devil! These

Presbyterians want no bishops at all! Presbyterians would run all by committee, made up of themselves! They claim the King must be subject to the word of the Church. That is, to them. What, a king subject to a committee of fanatics? He could be removed! That is the path to anarchy and revolution. What stops it? The beauty of the Church of England, its great arch of bishops and archbishops, who accept the King is Head of the Church, appointed by God. I tell you: no bishops, no king!

He stands. They all kneel, heads bowed.

I will be blunt. And will, I warn you, if provoked, be bloody. I will have no talk of presbyteries, not one word! Only if I grow idle, lazy, fat, and senile and insane, why, then, I will set up a presbytery! Now think on!

JAMES *abruptly leaves his chair and exits.*

The DIVINES *slowly stand.*

CECIL (*to* ANDREWES *and* REYNOLDS). I thought that went very well.

They stare at CECIL *who makes to exit then stays to overhear.*

BARROW. We have done God's work here! God's work! The Antichrist's Church will fall!

BARROW *is shunned by the* DIVINES *who exit by one door, he by another.*

ANDREWES *and* REYNOLDS *alone, but for* CECIL *watching them from a distance.*

ANDREWES. Why did you allow that wild man Barrow to come with you?

REYNOLDS. He speaks for many.

ANDREWES. But not for us, Reynolds. You and I may dis-agree on many matters...

REYNOLDS. We do. Altar rails. Take away the altar rails in church and we would have more agreement.

ANDREWES. Why are Puritans so obsessed with altar rails?

REYNOLDS. They are the symbol of priestly power. The priest
stands behind the altar rail to give communion. He puts
himself nearer to God than ordinary men. But we are all
equal before the Almighty, no matter what robes we wear...

ANDREWES. Yes yes, but...

REYNOLDS. The rails are an abomination! Rip them out from
all the churches in the land!

ANDREWES. Dear God. Are we going to tear each other apart
in this country over a minor feature of church architecture?

REYNOLDS. 'Dear God', indeed.

They pause.

ANDREWES. Doctor Reynolds, my point is that though you
and I disagree...

REYNOLDS. Passionately...

ANDREWES. ... at times passionately, we are moderate men.
But His Majesty has bundled us all together as fanatics.
(*Lower*.) He is a king and, at heart, all kings are...
(*Hesitates*.)

REYNOLDS. Tyrants?

They look at each other.

We must ask to speak to him.

ANDREWES. But without your extremists.

REYNOLDS. And without yours.

They exit.

Scene Two

Enter JAMES *clutching* ANNE*'s coronation dress in one hand. It trails upon the ground. In the other hand he has a flagon of wine.*

GEORGE *enters, also with a flagon of wine, and on an unsteady line across the stage.*

CECIL *lurks to overhear.*

GEORGE. You peppered them!

JAMES. I did I did.

GEORGE. Peppered!

JAMES. If we had been in school, I the teacher, they the schoolboys, I'd have plied the rod on their buttocks! Thwack thwack!

GEORGE. Thwack thwack!

JAMES. I played them, I diddled and dazed.

GEORGE. You flayed their flabby behinds! It was a triumph.

JAMES *stops and stares.*

JAMES. 'Triumph'? No. No… no no.

GEORGE. You are the conquering hero.

JAMES. No. These people are fractious, they will break, they will splinter, they will tear.

GEORGE. 'Tear'…

JAMES. It's not secure, George. The country. Not stable.

GEORGE. But you are wildly popular, thousands in the streets shouting your name, the country's *en fête*… As the French have it.

JAMES. Passing show. The ground will split the length of England, a great divide, and the house the Tudors built, monarchy, Church, all of it, will fall into the abyss.

GEORGE. My dear, too much wine makes you think apocalypse.

JAMES. No. In wine, reality. (*The dress in his fist.*) I must talk to that woman!

GEORGE. What woman?

JAMES (*raises the dress*). This woman! The whore who changed England!

GEORGE. If you want to talk to her, first you'll have to find her head. Ha!

JAMES does not find that funny.

JAMES. Get out.

GEORGE. What?

JAMES. Go!

GEORGE. My dear heart...

JAMES. I am not your dear heart, I am your dread Sovereign and Liege Majesty and I want your arse out of my sight!

GEORGE. Oh! Oh!

GEORGE turns, and runs off in tears.

JAMES. Anne. Anne. Tell me what you began and I will end it.

He turns and is going as ANNE enters. She is wearing night-clothes. They pass each other, without eye contact. He holds out the dress. She takes it.

Exit JAMES.

Scene Three

ANNE *staggers and sinks to the ground, hugging the dress to her.*

Enter LADY ROCHFORD, *running,* CELIA *and* JANE.

ROCHFORD. My Lady, you should be in bed…

ANNE. No, I want to go to the forest.

ROCHFORD. Anne, please.

ANNE. Farnham Forest, there's a wise man there.

ROCHFORD. You have a fever! Back into bed, now.

ANNE. The man in the forest tells me about God.

Enter HENRY, CROMWELL *behind, and behind him* SLOOP *and* SIMPKIN.

HENRY *stands over* ANNE. *Everyone else backs away.* HENRY *is very gentle in this scene, no trace of anger.*

HENRY. My love.

ANNE. Have you come to take it away?

HENRY. Take away what, my love?

ANNE. My dress.

HENRY. Why should I do that?

ANNE. Because I was made Queen in it. And now they won't let me be Queen any more.

LADY ROCHFORD *starts forward.*

ROCHFORD. Sire, the Queen is feverish after the birth…

HENRY *waves her away. He stoops and takes* ANNE *in his arms.*

HENRY. You know me, Anne?

She looks at him. He strokes her face.

ANNE. My Lord, I... I was at my coronation, the great pillars
   of the Abbey all around me, and they became trees, and I
   was in a forest talking to... (*Stops.*) A man. Some man. I
   don't know.

HENRY. The child is healthy. I am going to call her Elizabeth,
   after her two grandmothers.

ANNE. You've seen her?

HENRY. Oh, yes, the midwives brought her to me. She has eyes
   like mine.

ANNE. She is not. She is not...

HENRY. There is time, Anne. We are still young.

He kisses her lips. He stands and turns to the others.

(*Publicly. Smiling.*) By the Grace of God this day, is born the
   Princess Elizabeth! And Her Majesty the Queen and I are
   still young, we are still young!

Applause, music, HENRY *sweeps away and exits.*

ANNE. Dress me.

ROCHFORD. Your Majesty, I don't think...

ANNE. Dress me. I want the Court to see me. I want them to
   see I'm joyful and healthy and me. Me.

LADY ROCHFORD *helps her to her feet. They all exit.*

Scene Four

Enter CROMWELL, SIMPKIN *and* SLOOP. SIMPKIN *has a portable writing tray around his neck and is reading a paper, quill in hand.*

CROMWELL. Read that back.

SIMPKIN. 'Where by sundry old histories and chronicles…'

CROMWELL. '…old *authentic* histories and chronicles…'

SIMPKIN. 'Where by divers sundry old authentic histories and chronicles, it is manifestly declared and expressed that this realm of England is an Empire governed by one Supreme Head and King…'

CROMWELL. No no, stiffen that up '…that this realm of England is an Empire…' then put in '…and so has been accepted in the world…'

SIMPKIN *and* SLOOP *look at each other, exhausted.*

What?

SLOOP. We thought a little time for dinner…

CROMWELL. We are cutting down the Pope's power in England and all you can think of is dinner?

SIMPKIN. The smells of the kitchen do come up the stairs…

SLOOP. Roast hog. Little squirts of fat through the crackling…

CROMWELL *stares at him.*

I can see… the little… squirts.

CROMWELL. I know your kind. The 'get away with as little as you can' Englishman. You'd have the country at dinner all day. Where would we be then?

SLOOP (*low*). Happier?

CROMWELL. What did you say?

SLOOP. Nothing nothing, sir.

CROMWELL. And on.

He paces, muttering phrases to himself.

SLOOP (*aside*). Now it's work every hour and through the night with him. And he's got a finger in everything. He's an MP, he's the King's manager in Parliament, he's a member of the King's Council, he's Receiver General, he's Master of the King's Jewel House, he's Master of the Court of Wards, and to top it all he's the Chancellor of the Exchequer.

CROMWELL (*stops*). Read that back.

SIMPKIN. 'Where by divers sundry old authentic histories and chronicles, it is manifestly declared...'

HENRY *enters at pace.* SIMPKIN *and* SLOOP *kneel,* CROMWELL *bows.*

CROMWELL/SIMPKIN/SLOOP. Your Majesty.

HENRY (*beaming*). The Queen is well.

CROMWELL. Thanks be to Almighty God.

HENRY. The child is healthy. The Princess Elizabeth. She has eyes like mine!

CROMWELL. She will adorn the future.

HENRY. And the Queen is well and going about the Court.

CROMWELL. The country will be overjoyed.

HENRY. 'Joy' is the word she herself has used. She says she is joyful and healthy.

CROMWELL. And you are both still young.

HENRY *stops beaming. A sticky moment.*

HENRY. Is that the Act?

CROMWELL. In draft, Sire.

HENRY. When will it be finished?

CROMWELL. Tonight, Sire, and Parliament will pass it tomorrow.

HENRY. Let me see.

The kneeling SIMPKIN *holds out the paper to* HENRY, *who snatches it from him. He stares at the paper for a moment.*

'Where by divers sundry old authentic histories…' Legal language, like falling off a horse into brambles. Cut me through this.

CROMWELL. As discussed with Your Majesty, the Act forbids all appeals to the Pope in Rome on religious or other matters. It makes Your Majesty the final legal authority in England, Wales and all your possessions.

HENRY. Well, good. (*A moment.*) And how do you argue that?

CROMWELL. By…

HENRY. It must be argued, truly and justly. All the world must see the truth and justice.

CROMWELL (*aside*). He's nervous. When he's like this the tactic is: get him to the dinner table quick as possible. (*To* HENRY.) The Act argues, rightly, that England is an Empire. And the English Crown is an Imperial Crown.

HENRY. I am an Emperor?

CROMWELL. Yes, Your Majesty. The line of the English Crown goes back to Brutus and the Fall of Troy.

HENRY. Really? Who says so?

CROMWELL. Your historians, Your Majesty.

HENRY. Well paid, no doubt. So, since I am an Emperor…

CROMWELL…. Your command over your Empire is absolute.

HENRY. You are certain of this, Cromwell?

CROMWELL. It's historical fact, Sire. Truth is power.

HENRY. The other way round, I think: power is truth.

> HENRY *beams at them. They realise he has made a joke and laugh dutifully.*

CROMWELL. Your Majesty. (*Bows. An unsteady step.*) Oh… my stomach.

HENRY. What's the matter?

CROMWELL. Forgive me, Sire. We have been working all day… the kitchens are just below these rooms…

HENRY. And you smell dinner! (*Laughs.*) Are you human after all, Thomas?

CROMWELL. None of us can work at Your Majesty's pace.

HENRY. I am not certain of the historical justification for the Act.

CROMWELL. It does have consequences. For example: since Your Majesty's person is Imperial, under the Act all Church charges and fees will go to you, not to Rome.

HENRY. Charges and fees?

CROMWELL. Church tithes, profits from monastic harvests and industries. Thousands of pounds.

HENRY. Thousands.

> *A moment.*

CROMWELL. New ships for Your Majesty's Navy.

> HENRY *pauses. He smiles. Makes a gesture, wafting his hand to his nose.*

HENRY. A good honest hog, turning on the spit. Fat spitting through the crackling. Come, let's all go to dinner.

> SIMPKIN *and* SLOOP *are enthusiastic.*

CROMWELL. If Your Majesty will excuse me, I will finish drafting the Act.

SIMPKIN *and* SLOOP *are appalled.*

HENRY (*to* SIMPKIN *and* SLOOP, *smiling*). Gentlemen, you are not coming to table yet.

They bow.

SIMPKIN. Your Majesty.

SLOOP. Your Majesty.

HENRY. You are a good servant, Thomas.

CROMWELL (*bows*). Your Majesty.

HENRY. So: after the Fall of Troy, Prince Aeneas sails to Italy and founds Rome, and Roman Emperors found my throne. Therefore I am Imperial. Well, it will do, it will do. I'll have trenchers and ale sent up to you.

SIMPKIN. Thank you, Your Majesty!

SLOOP. Your Majesty!

HENRY *exits. Relief.*

CROMWELL. Right. Continue.

SIMPKIN. 'If any person or persons provoke or secure any manner of appeals to the Bishop of Rome, or to the See of Rome, or do procure or execute any manner of process from the See of Rome, to the derogation or let of the due execution of this Act…'

CROMWELL. Wait. After 'the See of Rome', insert '…or by authority thereof…'

SIMPKIN. 'The See of Rome' is mentioned twice… insert after which…

CROMWELL. Oh… read it again.

SIMPKIN (*sagging*). 'If any person or persons…'

Enter ANNE *at pace. They bow.*

CROMWELL. Your Majesty.

SIMPKIN. Your Majesty.

SLOOP. Your Majesty.

ANNE (*to* CROMWELL, *low*). Sir.

She turns away.

CROMWELL (*to* SIMPKIN *and* SLOOP). When it arrives, have your food next door.

SIMPKIN. Sir.

SLOOP. Sir.

As they go.

The mood has changed.

SIMPKIN. You know why. The milch cow's dropped the wrong kind of calf.

SLOOP *giggles.* ANNE *whirls round and stares at them. They bow and exit.*

ANNE. Is the Act ready?

CROMWELL. It will be with Parliament tomorrow.

ANNE. He's nervous about it.

CROMWELL. Yes.

ANNE *falters.*

Ma'am, are you…

ANNE. Don't fuss. (*A moment, then she smiles.*) Taking the Pope's money. He'll excommunicate us all, won't he.

CROMWELL. Oh, in the end he'll send the whole country to Hell.

ANNE. Well, that will be merry.

CROMWELL. You think so?

ANNE. It'll be the Gates of Heaven that will open to England, Thomas, not Hell! And we will dance and be merry, in the true Faith.

CROMWELL. I pray for that.

ANNE. I too.

CROMWELL. But we are on a stony path. There will have to be another Act of Parliament, to secure the succession of the Princess Elizabeth.

ANNE. And make a bastard of Catherine's child?

CROMWELL. Yes.

ANNE. Needs be.

CROMWELL. Then we will have to have an Act making His Majesty Supreme Head of the Church of England.

ANNE (*irritated*). Needs be needs be.

CROMWELL. And there may be blood.

ANNE. We are conspirators for Christ. Maybe it was like this for the Apostles, on the shores of Galilee, whispering secretly in a room. Planning to save the whole world.

CROMWELL. Perhaps.

ANNE. I must dine with His Majesty. Though I could do without pork.

She turns to go.

CROMWELL. A friend of ours is in England again.

ANNE *stops.*

I want to make him an offer.

ANNE. Then meet him.

CROMWELL. I think you should.

A pause.

ANNE. When I talked to Master Tyndale, I… felt a kind of peace. I think he's a Saint. Though we're not going to have Saints any more, are we.

CROMWELL. He's a good man. Though the good can be a burden.

ANNE. I'll see him.

CROMWELL. But be careful, Ma'am. If Thomas More got hold of him, he'd burn him. I couldn't stop that, I'm not powerful enough.

ANNE. Not yet, Thomas. (*A moment.*) What offer?

Break the scene.

CROMWELL *exits.* ANNE *remains on the stage.*

Scene Five

CELIA *and* JANE *come on with a cloak and a riding whip. They hand them to* ANNE, *then exit.*

ANNE *stands alone on the stage.*

Then, seeming to have appeared from nowhere, TYNDALE, *the two* COUNTRY WOMEN *and two* COUNTRY MEN *are there.*

A silence, all of them still.

Then TYNDALE *bows.*

TYNDALE. Your Majesty.

ANNE. Master Tyndale.

ANNE *turns and glares at the four* COUNTRY PEOPLE. *The* MEN *bow, the* WOMEN *curtsy, raggedly. They are hostile.*

COUNTRY PEOPLE. Your Majesty.

ANNE. I bring you an offer.

FIRST COUNTRY MAN. What can the likes of you offer a Christian man?

TYNDALE. No, John. (*To* ANNE.) An offer, Ma'am?

ANNE. I have been asked to enquire whether you would consent to be a member of the King's Council.

Disbelief.

TYNDALE. The King's Council?

ANNE. Yes.

TYNDALE. A Privy Councillor, me?

ANNE. Yes.

The SECOND COUNTRY WOMAN *laughs.*

TYNDALE. This offer is from His Majesty?

ANNE. It's from a powerful man.

TYNDALE. Meaning the King?

ANNE. No one can speak directly for His Majesty.

FIRST COUNTRY WOMAN. She means it's from Thomas Cromwell.

FIRST COUNTRY MAN. This is Satan's mire, Court politics…

TYNDALE. And what would Sir Thomas More say about me, the heretic Protestant, whispering in the King's ear?

ANNE. His Majesty greatly respects you.

TYNDALE. More wants to burn me. Which I do take to heart: he is Lord Chancellor of England.

ANNE. For now.

TYNDALE. Ah. Satan's mire.

ANNE. Think of it, Master Tyndale. You would take the Word of Christ to the heart of Government.

TYNDALE. And what word would that be, through the King's ear, to the heart of England?

ANNE. That is for your conscience...

TYNDALE. It would be: 'Oh King, oh King, you were wrong to divorce your wife.'

FIRST COUNTRY WOMAN (*claps her hands*). Oh! Praise Jesus you said it to her face!

ANNE *glares at her. A pause.*

ANNE. No.

TYNDALE. 'Oh King, take back your true wife, Catherine.'

FIRST COUNTRY WOMAN. True Queen!

ANNE. No. Leviticus 20, verse 21: 'If a man shall take his brother's wife, it is an unclean thing: he hath uncovered his brother's nakedness: they shall be childless.'

TYNDALE. Deuteronomy 25, verse 2: 'If brethren dwell together, and one of them die, and have no child...'

ANNE. No no...

TYNDALE. '...the wife of the dead shall not marry without unto a stranger...'

ANNE. No no no...

TYNDALE. '...her husband's brother shall go unto her, and take her to him to wife, and perform the duties of an husband's brother unto her...'

ANNE. No no no, no, yes but... With Catherine, he was Catholic! With me he is... new, a new King. Of a new England, reformed, truly Christian. Isn't that what God wants?

TYNDALE. We can only be guided by His Word.

ANNE. But what is His Word? Leviticus or Deuteronomy?

TYNDALE. There must be interpretation. Leviticus refers to taking a brother's wife when the brother is still living.

ANNE. Nowhere does it say that.

TYNDALE. That is the revealed meaning.

ANNE. Revealed how?

TYNDALE. By prayer.

ANNE. Oh, then let's pray and make anything true! We're cutting free of the Pope in England, because of me. Me! Don't you understand that? Because I'm Queen.

> TYNDALE *turns away, distressed.*

SECOND COUNTRY WOMAN. You're no Queen of England.

ANNE. How dare you!

SECOND COUNTRY WOMAN. Ooh ooh, Your Majesty. (*Mocking bow.*) Going to have me hauled to Tyburn for treason, have me hanged and cut down, my innards burnt at front of me, have me cut into quarters?

FIRST COUNTRY WOMAN. That's what they should do to you, strumpet.

FIRST COUNTRY MAN. Concubine of Babylon.

SECOND COUNTRY MAN. You're a whore.

SECOND COUNTRY WOMAN. Witch.

> *One of them picks up a stone to throw at* ANNE.

TYNDALE. Stop this, stop it!

> *A pause.*

ANNE. Is there any hope you may change your opinion?

TYNDALE. It's not my opinion, it's God's Word.

ANNE. But if... if the King... put me aside, declared Catherine his lawful wife, she'd have her Catholic way. She's a very strong woman.

TYNDALE. As are you.

ANNE. She'd give the English Church back to the Pope. Do you want that?

TYNDALE. No. Course not.

ANNE. Then join us. Guide the King. Help us build a new Jerusalem.

TYNDALE. Your Majesty. Against what the world says, I think you have Christ within you. But the King must take back his true wife.

ANNE. But you call me 'Majesty'!

FIRST COUNTRY WOMAN. He's polite.

ANNE. Can't you see? With me, the Reformation lives. With Catherine it would die.

TYNDALE. God will work his purpose out.

ANNE. Through me!

TYNDALE. Tell Thomas Cromwell 'no'. (*Turns away.*)

ANNE. I love the King. I love him.

> *The* SECOND COUNTRY WOMAN *snorts.*

> Go on, go on, sneer, say filthy things. But I love the King and he loves me and that's how God works. Works His purpose, His way, through our love.

SECOND COUNTRY WOMAN. Stewing in an adulterous bed…?

ANNE. That's all I have, the King's love. It protects me from all the… viciousness, the plots at Court, the Spanish spies, Sir Thomas More, even from you, Master Tyndale. Because that love comes from God. Can't you see that? Can't you see that?

TYNDALE. Madam, we must be our own confessors. Best you look into your heart. Good day to you.

ANNE. No…

TYNDALE *and the* COUNTRY MEN *and* WOMEN *walk away.*

Can't we say a prayer? Can't we sing?

They exit.

(*Aside.*) Look into my heart. But I do. I do.

She turns away and exits.

Scene Six

Enter JAMES *and* CECIL, PARROT *and* GEORGE *at a distance.* SERVANTS *follow, bringing on the velvet chair.* JAMES *sprawls in it.*

JAMES. Are they outside?

CECIL. They have been for five hours.

JAMES. Left alone together? Standing up?

CECIL. As you instructed, Sire, we removed the chairs from the chamber.

JAMES. Good. Has there been sound of disputation?

CECIL. There was some shouting in the first hour but they have quietened.

JAMES. And no food, no drink. Good good. Did you allow a break for a pish?

CECIL. I thought, for dignity's sake…

JAMES. Pity pity. Full bladders can move mountains. (*Laughs.*) Right right. I'll talk only to the leaders. Pull 'em! Pull 'em! Pull 'em in!

CECIL. Master Parrot.

CECIL *nods to* PARROT, *who bows and turns to leave.*

PARROT (*aside*). Funny thing about Anglicans and Puritans: the Anglicans have a musty whiff about 'em. But the Puritans have a strange stink. I think it's the lack of alcohol.

He exits.

JAMES (*to* CECIL). Have you found the grave?

CECIL. With difficulty. Yes. It was as if she never lived. But finally we found a record in the Tower's old files. It would seem she was executed, in the Tower, on the green beside the Chapel of St Peter ad Vincula. The body and the head were then put into a chest and buried under the floor of the Chapel.

JAMES. A chest! Shall we dig it up?

CECIL. I think, Sire, that would be... seen by your subjects as rather strange.

JAMES. Oh, Robert, whoops slip-slop, I forgot. You have no imagination.

CECIL. Sometimes I count it as a blessing that I don't.

Enter ANDREWES *and* REYNOLDS, *exhausted. They kneel.*

PARROT. Dean Andrewes and Doctor Reynolds.

JAMES. Dean Andrewes, Doctor Reynolds, I believe you asked to see me. Please, do stand.

Wearily, they get to their feet.

Well? Well?

ANDREWES. After much prayer and contemplation, and dispute amongst ourselves, we we...

REYNOLDS. We need a new Bible.

A pause.

JAMES. A new Bible.

ANDREWES. Newly translated.

REYNOLDS. A translation to end all translations.

CECIL. Your Majesty, that will surely mean the most divisive, argumentative falling out over every verse of Scripture…

JAMES. No no no no. (*Falls silent.*) Hum hum hum. Ha! (*Falls silent.*) Ah ah. Hah! Hah! Hip hah! Hah! (*Falls silent, sprawled, with a vacant stare.*)

ANDREWES (*to* CECIL). Should we leave him…

CECIL. No no. Wait.

A silence.

JAMES (*snaps back into life*). How will you translate the Greek word '*Ecclesia*'?

ANDREWES. Church.

REYNOLDS. Congregation.

JAMES. Hah hah! A world of difference. 'Church' meaning an institution of the State. 'Congregation' meaning a meeting, higgledy-di-piggledy group. Nub, gentlemen. Nub. And another, nubbly knobbly nub. How to translate '*Presbyteros*'?

ANDREWES. Priest.

REYNOLDS. Elder.

JAMES. 'Priest', ordained by a bishop, but 'elder'? An older man in a meeting. And in St Paul's Corinthians, the Greek word '*Agape*'? Faith, hope and…

ANDREWES. Charity.

REYNOLDS. Love.

JAMES. 'Charity', yes, public responsibility, alms, civic rectitude. But 'love' can go anywhere, lead to loose talk of the love of God and this and that, a path to heresy and darkness. Hu, hu, hum. Hop!

He falls silent. Unease amongst the listeners.

In my Bible there will be: 'church', 'priest' and 'charity'.

REYNOLDS. I...

They stare at REYNOLDS. *But he bows.*

JAMES. And you will take, as the first source, the translation of
William Tyndale.

ANDREWES. The heretic Bible? We've burnt it all these
years...

JAMES. It is the best. I read it every night.

REYNOLDS. It shines with God's Word.

ANDREWES. But Tyndale has 'congregation', 'elder' and
'love' throughout!

JAMES. Then rewrite him, Dean. Rewrite. Make him safe for
good Anglicans to read. (*Stands.*) Gentlemen, I invite you
and your long-suffering companions next door, to sit with me
at dinner.

ANDREWES. To sit would be a boon, Sire.

JAMES (*smiles*). Would it now, Dean. (*Waves them away.*)

ANDREWES. Your Majesty. (*Bows.*)

REYNOLDS. Your Majesty. (*Bows.*)

They go to exit but just before they do, a group of DIVINES
come on and surround them, anxious for news.

ANDREWES. I will insist on the best scholars of the age, and
poets.

REYNOLDS. Poets?

ANDREWES. For the odd felicitous phrase. I will summon
John Donne. His Majesty has decided that...

They all exit.

Enter GEORGE.

JAMES. We will have committees, but of a kind I can control!
Piles of committees, of them all, Puritans Anglicans, closet
Catholics, religiosity in all its hues, piled high! And push and

pull them, let piles of divines totter and sway! And do the work. And bind us all together with a Bible. Because bound we must be. Good. Good. Good. (*Stands.*) Now, let's go to dinner and get them all drunk. (*To* GEORGE.) Come, George! A wager! Which kind of divine will we get into a woman's dress first? Anglican or Puritan?

GEORGE. Neither, I fear.

JAMES. Pessimism, George! Pessimism-issy-miss, ban it! We will translate a Bible and transform England. Dinner dinner dinner!

They move to go off.

Enter ANNE, *in her nightdress, clutching her coronation dress. She sinks to the floor.*

JAMES *stops. They stare at each other for a moment. He stumbles.*

GEORGE, CECIL *and* PARROT *rush to him.*

CECIL. Your Majesty, are you ill?

JAMES. No no. A shadow. (*Sudden anger.*) Well, come on come on! Let's stuff these bastards full of my food!

He storms away and exits.

CECIL *and* GEORGE *look at each other.*

CECIL. What is it? Can you tell me?

GEORGE. He's fighting something in his head.

CECIL. In his head? How can you fight in your head?

GEORGE. He can.

CECIL. And the fight's between…

GEORGE. Don't you know that, My Lord? With all your spies and schemes and sophistication? It's a war between two Englands.

They exit.

Scene Seven

The Chapel of St Peter ad Vincula in the Tower of London.

GUARD (*offstage*). His Majesty will enter the Chapel! His
Majesty is not to be disturbed!

A moment.

Guard! To salute!

Enter JAMES. *He has a flagon of wine. His shirt is hanging
out. He carves a long, curving line across the stage and falls
down. He rights the flagon just in time.*

JAMES. The Tower of London. Buried you here. In a chapel.
Hid you away under the floor. (*Knocks on the floor.*) Anne.
Anne, who pulled you down? Who... who... (*Passes out.*)

Scene Eight

The unconscious JAMES *lying on the stage.*

Enter CROMWELL *and* SIMPKIN.

CROMWELL. On the hour!

SIMPKIN. Yes, My Lord.

CROMWELL. Reports of His Majesty. What he says, his mood,
looks, sighs. On the hour!

SIMPKIN. Yes, My Lord.

They exit.

Enter LADY ROCHFORD, CELIA *and* JANE.

ANNE. Where is it?

ROCHFORD. With the midwives.

ANNE. What was it?

They stare at her, horrified.

A boy, yes? A boy.

They still cannot speak.

Don't let him see it. Where did the midwives put it?

CELIA. In a bowl by the...

ANNE. Get it get it!

CELIA rushes off.

Enter HENRY with a bowl covered by a bloodstained cloth. He holds it still, looking at it.

Enter CROMWELL, followed by SIMPKIN and SLOOP.

SIMPKIN. Your Majesty, it would be best not...

CROMWELL. Let him.

HENRY lifts the cloth and stares. He freezes with horror.

CROMWELL gestures to SIMPKIN, who comes forward quickly and takes the bowl from HENRY's hands.

SIMPKIN, with SLOOP, takes the bowl to a far corner of the stage.

HENRY cannot move.

HENRY. Why does God do this?

CROMWELL. If Your Majesty... wishes to pray with me?

HENRY. 'Pray'? I don't want to pray. I want to know why! Why!?

He lurches away and exits.

SIMPKIN lifts the cloth on the bowl. He and SLOOP stare.

SIMPKIN. It's got gills. And flippers.

They giggle.

SLOOP. That's what she's given England. (*Laughs.*) Fortune's wheel.

CROMWELL. Throw that thing in the cesspit. Now!

SIMPKIN *replaces the cloth. He and* SLOOP *are about to exit.*

And no talk of the Wheel of Fortune, all that crap, there's no fortune, no fate. Just the eye of God in Heaven staring down on what we do, crawling on this Earth! We are what we do!

They hesitate.

Go on, get out!

SLOOP. Yes, My Lord.

SIMPKIN. Yes, My Lord. (*To* SLOOP.) A wobble.

SLOOP. The Wheel of Fortune is wobbly.

They exit.

CROMWELL *remains on the stage.*

Scene Nine

ANNE, LADY ROCHFORD *and* JANE *are still onstage.*

Enter CELIA, *distressed.*

CELIA. Ma'am, I couldn't stop the midwives, they…

ANNE. He saw it? Oh, God in Heaven…

Enter HENRY.

LADY ROCHFORD, CELIA *and* JANE *curtsy.*

ROCHFORD / CELIA / JANE. Your Majesty.

He waves them away. They move quickly and regroup, trying to overhear.

ANNE. Do you hate me?

HENRY. No.

ANNE. It is hateful.

HENRY. No.

ANNE. I am hateful.

HENRY. No no, my love.

He kneels and embraces her.

ANNE. What does it mean?

HENRY. I don't know, Anne.

ANNE. It can't be God's Will, Henry. It can't.

HENRY. If it is, we will bear it.

ANNE. No no, He wants you to have a son.

HENRY. Then you will give me one.

ANNE. What if I can't?

HENRY. Then that is God's Will and we will bear it.

ANNE. I will give you a son.

HENRY. Yes.

ANNE. Yes.

A moment.

HENRY. Oh, to be alone with you.

ANNE. 'On some unhaunted isle.

HENRY. Obscure from all society,
    From love and hate…

ANNE. From love and hate and worldly foes.'

HENRY (*smiles, settling her against him*). Well, worldly foes you have seen off, my love. Two Chancellors of England, Wolsey, Thomas More… 'I have lain their heads at your feet.' Could be a lyric in there.

> 'Her rival's rosy head,
> Lain upon my true love's bed'… (*Laughs.*)

ANNE. We should not be coarse about God's Will.

HENRY. No no.

ANNE. You believe it was God's Will?

A moment.

HENRY. Forget the island in the song. Oh, to be just a man and a woman in a room, in each other's arms.

ANNE. But we're not just a man and a woman. We're a king and a queen.

HENRY. Really? Is that what they say about us out there?

They kiss, long and gently.

He stands.

I'll leave you to your ladies, you must rest. And be well for the May Day tournament. You will be my Lady, my Champion will have your favour, you will have my gift from him, your flag will fly with mine.

ANNE (*bows her head*). My Lord.

HENRY *goes to* LADY ROCHFORD, CELIA *and* JANE.

HENRY. Attend to Her Majesty.

LADY ROCHFORD, CELIA *and* JANE *curtsy*.

ROCHFORD / CELIA / JANE. Your Majesty.

HENRY. Lady Jane.

JANE (*curtsies again*). Your Majesty.

A smile between them and HENRY *exits, fast.*

LADY ROCHFORD *and* CELIA *turn and look at* JANE.

What? What?

LADY ROCHFORD *and* CELIA *go to* ANNE. *The three of them exit.*

Scene Ten

JANE *alone.*

Enter LADY ROCHFORD. *She gives* JANE *a letter and exits.*

JANE *reads some of the letter.*

JANE. Oh! (*Hides the letter.*)

   Enter CROMWELL.

CROMWELL. The King sent you a letter.

JANE. I… don't know.

CROMWELL. Please, don't play the stupid little girl just because you are a stupid little girl. He sent you a letter.

JANE. Yes.

CROMWELL. Are you going to reply?

JANE. I…

CROMWELL. Do reply.

JANE. My Lord…

CROMWELL. A warning. When you are with him do not discuss matters of religion or state. Show him your bosoms, not your opinions.

   She is shocked. She runs away and exits.

Scene Eleven

Loud music. Cheers and shouts, offstage.

Enter HENRY *and* CROMWELL. SLOOP *is in attendance. Urgency.*

Enter LADY ROCHFORD, *who hovers, anxious.*

HENRY. Leave the tournament, while it is in full flow? What are you thinking of, Cromwell?

CROMWELL. There is a threat to Your Majesty.

HENRY. What threat?

CROMWELL. It is too terrible for Your Majesty to hear in so public a place.

HENRY. Some vague threat and I leave the tourney? Like fleeing a battlefield? No.

CROMWELL. Your Majesty, in all the years I've served you, was I right about Wolsey and his letters to the Pope? Was I right about Thomas More's treason? Sire, your life is in danger, let me protect it.

A pause.

HENRY. Oh, well well, tournaments aren't what they used to be, no one really gets hurt any more. Not like in the good old days. We'll leave. Bring Her Majesty. (*Turns to go.*)

CROMWELL. Best Her Majesty does not go with you.

HENRY. Why?

CROMWELL. For security. She will follow in another coach.

HENRY. You really are worried, Cromwell. It makes you... smaller. (*Produces a gold cloth embroidered with the King's arms.*) Give this to Her Majesty. It was to be the gift to her from my Champion, after his victory. Which was, of course, certain. (*Laughs and is leaving.*) Give it to her with my love.

CROMWELL (*taking the cloth*). Your Majesty.

Exit HENRY.

Enter SIMPKIN, *with* JANE.

His Majesty is leaving. Go with him. Now!

JANE. I...

CROMWELL (*shouts*). Attend His Majesty. Now!

JANE *exits, running.*

SIMPKIN. Lady Jane is a little Catholic.

CROMWELL. Lady Jane Seymour has the arse, tits and hips for the job. That is all His Majesty will bother with. I think he's had enough of politicking women. (*Closes his eyes for a moment, exhausted. Then, to* LADY ROCHFORD.) Get her.

ROCHFORD. I can't do this.

CROMWELL (*turns on her*). This morning you swore an affidavit, that your mistress is a whore, has slept even with a no doubt pox-ridden musician of the Court, along with five other men.

ROCHFORD. Maybe I was mistaken.

CROMWELL. Mistaken? You told me and other witnesses you saw her humping on a bed with your own husband! Were you mistaken in that?

ROCHFORD. I can't, she's... been so kind.

CROMWELL. Oh, 'kind'! Good, then let kindness rule. Let's be kind to the King of Spain, the King of France, the Pope, the thieving, child-raping monks in the monasteries, let's do nothing about the broken, dangerous world, and die, cut to pieces, but kind.

ROCHFORD. I hate politics.

CROMWELL. Really? I love 'em. You want to unswear this affidavit, fine, fine, but then, My Lady Rochford, as you are the bawd who pimped the Boleyn whore men, your husband and for all I know your own body, you know what I will do to you?

SIMPKIN (*worried*). My Lord…

CROMWELL. I will have a rope put about your head, with knots at your eyes, and tighten that rope until you swear again! Do I make myself clear? Now get your whore of a mistress.

LADY ROCHFORD *exits, in tears and running.*

(*Turns on* SIMPKIN.) And what is the matter with you?

SIMPKIN. Nothing, My Lord.

CROMWELL. Not feeling something, are you, Simpkin?

SIMPKIN. No, My Lord.

CROMWELL. Good man.

ANNE *and* LADY ROCHFORD *enter.* LADY ROCHFORD *steps away from her.*

Madam, you are under arrest for treason.

Enter GUARDS.

Say nothing!

ANNE. Where is His Majesty?

CROMWELL. I told you…

ANNE. What is this, Thomas?

CROMWELL. You have been found to be what you have always been, a treasonous whore.

She stares at him.

ANNE. Where is His Majesty?

CROMWELL. Don't you dare say his name. Your only hope for decent treatment is in silence.

Talking over each other.

ANNE. This is because of the money, isn't it –

CROMWELL. I cannot advise you more strongly to –

ANNE. – The money from the dissolving of the monasteries that you have stolen –

CROMWELL. – hold your whoring, witch's tongue –

ANNE. – You know I know –

CROMWELL. – You aren't hearing me –

ANNE. – I have it, nearly all of it, the sordid details –

CROMWELL. – Don't speak, just don't –

ANNE. – The houses you are building, gifts of monastery lands to your family, your favourites –

CROMWELL. – With every word you are nearer to Tyburn –

ANNE. – You think you can pull me down? I will give the King all the evidence –

CROMWELL. It is already on its way to him.

She stops.

ANNE. What is? The evidence…? What…

CROMWELL. Just take one thing that condemns you. You fornicated with your brother, her husband.

ANNE. What?

CROMWELL (*points at* LADY ROCHFORD). She has sworn it.

ANNE *turns to look at* LADY ROCHFORD, *who turns away and leans against a pillar, nauseous.*

ANNE. Jane?

ROCHFORD (*turns on her*). I just want to be alive.

ANNE. Jane, what of God's work?

ROCHFORD. God's work? They'd have put a rope round my eyes, that's God's work!

She runs away and exits.

ANNE. Thomas.

He stares at her.

All we've worked for. The Word in England. Please, I need to talk to the King…

CROMWELL. Keep mouthing about the King and you'll be torn to bits before the mob at Tyburn. Be silent and it'll be a discreet matter in the Tower.

ANNE *staggers, then backs away.*

ANNE. Let me see him. Please please. Let me see him. Henry! Henry! Please! Please! Please! Please! Please…

The GUARDS *pull her away, she goes limp, still screaming out, they have to drag her. They exit.*

CROMWELL. Right, Simpkin! Lots to do.

SIMPKIN *in difficulty.*

What's the matter with you?

SIMPKIN. Could I have it?

CROMWELL. Have what?

SIMPKIN. The Champion's gift, that was to be hers.

CROMWELL (*realises he still has it in his hand*). This? Here.

SIMPKIN *takes the cloth, kisses it and bursts into tears.*

Oh, for crying out loud.

SIMPKIN. I was in love with her.

CROMWELL. We were all in love with her.

SIMPKIN. Sorry.

CROMWELL. Don't worry.

SIMPKIN. Oh dear.

CROMWELL. Better now?

SIMPKIN. Yes, yes, My Lord. (*Sniffs, wipes his nose with his sleeve.*) It was her eyes.

CROMWELL. I know. She'd look straight at you and wasn't scared. What man could deal with that?

SIMPKIN. She'd be scared now.

CROMWELL. Yes. Fear is the great leveller. Now can we please do the paperwork?

They are going off, quickly.

I want all the confessions written out for His Majesty in a large, clear hand, he will rage and tear some up so have copies ready for him...

They exit.

Scene Twelve

JAMES *wakes with a shout.*

JAMES. Hah! Oh. (*Looks around.*) Where are you, woman? (*Knocks on the floor, puts his ear to the ground.*)

ANNE *enters up through the floor.*

ANNE. I'm over here. People always look for me in the wrong place.

A moment. They look at each other.

JAMES. You're the wine.

ANNE. You're what I saw in the thirteen seconds.

JAMES. Thirteen seconds...?

ANNE. While my head was in the straw. I saw my body. (*Giggles*.) No head! And I saw the people kneeling by the scaffold. And behind them, I saw you. (*Aside, to the audience*.) And you. The demons of the future.

JAMES (*drinks*). It was the money, wasn't it. That's why you fell.

ANNE. Men and the money.

JAMES (*finishes drinking, suppresses a hiccup*). I looked at the records of the dissolution of the monasteries. I saw how Cromwell filched thousands. I have an eye for accounts.

ANNE. The money was meant for schools, universities, houses for the relief of the poor. Cromwell stole it.

JAMES. You were going to tell King Henry.

ANNE. The last three weeks I was alive, I couldn't speak to Henry, couldn't send a message. Cromwell cut me off. While he told his lies. Oh, how I begged. (*Sing-song*.) Beg beg beg, funny how you do that, when you're going to die, you say you won't but you do. Beg beg beg. (*Smiles*.) But Henry was a good husband.

JAMES. Who had your head spin into the straw?

ANNE. When you were young and they came to you and told you they were going to execute your mother, what did you say?

    JAMES *is silent*.

    Royal families are different.

JAMES. You mean others only dream of cutting off the heads of wives and mothers?

ANNE. We have to do God's Will.

JAMES. If we know it. (*Drinks*.)

ANNE. We know His Will because we have His Word.

    JAMES *finishes drinking. He is sagging*.

JAMES. The Word, the one Word, God's Word, what is it?

ANNE. You don't know it because you're a demon.

JAMES. Demon?

ANNE. You all are in the future. Godless demons.

JAMES. Were you an… (*Slurs*.) insufferably holy cow when you were alive?

ANNE. Oh no, I had a lot of fun.

JAMES. I'm giving the future a new Bible! God's Word!

ANNE. Not God's, yours.

JAMES. God's Word my Word, God's Word my Word. My my my Word. I… Tell me this, Queen Anne, great Queen. (*Takes a great breath*.) Why… (*Takes another great breath*.) Why is it that all we do in the name of God is always exactly the same as what we need to do in our own self-interest?

ANNE. That is a demon thought.

JAMES (*grunt*). Hunh! Ha! Hunh.

With a great big snore he rolls over and passes out.

ANNE (*aside*). Dear demons of the future, what I can't tell… what I can't tell is what you believe. You're so strange to me, as I must be strange to you. Be careful of love. No, don't be careful. Why not live for love? Why not live for a better world?

Oh, I can't see you any more. And now you can't see me. Goodbye, demons. God bless you all.

She blows the audience a kiss.

The End.

? Joseph Harrington   late 18 artist
  or Harinton